World War II, to the Greatest Generation A Poetic History of the War's Duration

Most would claim they weren't so great.
True, but doing great things was their fate.

George L. Hand

iUniverse, Inc.
Bloomington

World War II, to the Greatest Generation
A Poetic History of the War's Duration
Most Vets would claim they weren't so great.
True, but doing great things was their fate,

iUniverse books may be ordered through booksellers or by contacting:

*iUniverse
1663 Liberty Drive
Bloomington, IN 47403
www.iuniverse.com
1-800-Authors (1-800-288-4677)*

*Because of the dynamic nature of the Internet, any web addresses or links
contained in this book may have changed since publication and may no longer be
valid. The views expressed in this work are solely those of the author and do not
necessarily reflect the views of the publisher, and the publisher hereby disclaims
any responsibility for them.*

*Any people depicted in stock imagery provided by Thinkstock are models,
and such images are being used for illustrative purposes only.*

Certain stock imagery © Thinkstock.

ISBN: 978-1-4620-7135-7 (sc)
ISBN: 978-1-4620-7136-4 (e)

Printed in the United States of America

iUniverse rev. date: 1/3/2012

Dedication

I dedicate this book to the veterans of World War II.
No words I have put together will ever do,
To honor what you did in your humble way.
You're the Greatest Generation to the end of days.

Acknowledgment

To all those unknown Wikipedia authors, I owe a debt.
You saved me uncounted hours and gallons of sweat.
I needed the facts. They were all there.
What a wonderful invention, so all can share.
There are literally thousands of books on World War II.
My favorite author is Steven Ambrose, several of his will do.
Interviews with participants provided a personal touch.
Several universities have verbal histories and such.
I wrote my book hoping it would help the young
Know what their fathers and other forebears had done.
Giving their all 'til that terrible war was won.

Table of Contents

Introduction

The biggest event in history was World War II
(Not counting the births and lives of only a few).
More countries were involved, more people as well.
The destruction was widespread with a continuous death
    knell.
The USA contributed the most in the Axis' defeat,
With our military force and our production fete.
I don't want to belittle the contribution of others.
Russians, Chinese, British and their commonwealth were our
    brothers.
I named but a few. More contributed a share
To defeat two evil empires in this affair.
This book of poems concerns Americans at war.
They gave their all, you couldn't ask for more.
It was such a vast undertaking, I've touched but a part.
Millions of stories are there, it's barely a start.
Some tales are fictional, while all are based on fact.
I've identified but few people in this tract.
Usually, I've used an initial or changed a name,
Since I don't want to bring any unwanted fame.
This is a humble tribute to our Greatest Generation.
For all time they should be held in total veneration.

Chapter 1. Retreat in the Pacific, 1941, 1942

1. Pearl Harbor

About the start of World War II, there's something to make
    clear.
Japan wanted to form "The Greater East Asia Co-prosperity
    Sphere."
The establishment of colonies was what they meant.
They'd provide material, to Japan this would be sent.
Then slave labor would man factory and mine.
For Japan the prosperity part was just fine.
They had invaded China as part of their plan.
President Roosevelt said stop or we'll place a ban.
We'll sell you no more scrap iron or oil.
This restriction made the Japanese military boil.
So they planned an attack to keep us at bay.
If they destroyed our Navy, we'd stay out of their way.
They wanted to invade colonies of the English, French, and
    Dutch.
There would be no opposition from us or not much.
We kept most of our Pacific fleet at Hawaiian bases.
The Japs figured we'd not dock ships at many other places.
As for strategy, their plan was well thought out.
They knew we were complacent. There was no doubt.
Japan's armada had six carriers with 414 planes.
Forty five other ships helped their victory to attain.
They moved their fleet in place for the attack.
They were lucky or they knew our security was slack.
If we had aircraft up on scouting duty, just a few,
Or any one believed the radar set that was new,
Their attack might have failed or had less cost,
And of ships, aircraft, and men we'd have had less lost.

But saying, "What if" is at most a senseless time waste.
World War II started for us with this foretaste.

2. Day of Infamy

"Hey, Sarge, take a look at the scope.
There's a bunch of blips, not serious I hope."
The military, whether enlisted or the top brass
Practices CYA, or translated, cover your ass.
"There's supposed to be B-17s coming in, an early flight.
Maybe that's what you see, at least it might.
I'll call it in. We'll go up the chain.
Nobody wants to be bothered. They'll think I'm a pain."
Sunday morning, what an ideal time to attack.
Some getting ready for church or golf, some still in the sack.
Everybody has something else to do in this idyllic place.
It's peacetime. No attack expected on any military base.
The Jap aircraft took off from carriers in their fleet.
Their planes flew in. No opposition did they meet.
Bombers and torpedo planes were in the first wave,
Wanting to send our battleships and carriers to the grave.
Fighters attacked our planes lined up on the ground.
Probably the easiest targets to ever be found.
The battleships were rocked as the torpedoes hit.
We see in our mind's eye a sailor with true grit.
A cook, no less, did what needed to be done.
He found ammunition and manned a machine gun.
Maybe his action was just being defiant,
But it showed that the Japs had wakened a sleeping giant.
They sunk four battleships and damaged four more.
188 aircraft were destroyed for those who keep score.
But three things the Japs missed that helped seal their fate.
All our aircraft carriers were at sea on that date.
They never touched our repair facilities or the fuel tanks.
So we were still able to refuel ships and repair those they sank.
One ship, the Arizona, remains where she lay,

A memorial to the 2400 killed that day.
The 'Day of Infamy' as we'll always remember Roosevelt say.

3. The Greatest Generation
The nation needed them, and they came forth
From village and city, the deep south and far north.
Most had never been out of the county of their birth.
They had never taken stock of their own self worth.
Their desires were straight forward. Have a decent life.
Check out the girls. Find one who'd be a good wife.
In time raise a family, be a man, work hard,
Be someone kith and kin would hold in high regard.
The biggest group of all the war's GIs
Were born in '23, which shouldn't be a surprise.
They all turned 18 the year the war began.
Shortly after, they volunteered almost every man.
Life had not been easy for many.
The depression years were hard, skimp every penny.
Some had left school to help their families get by.
Some were sent away. They could no longer be fed is why.
The country called. They did their part.
More died in battle from the very start.
After the war, the GI bill gave them a break,
A college education, skill training, opportunities to take.
Business loans, home purchase loans, and medical care,
The greatest piece of legislation, no other can compare.
For the most, as time passed, the normal life returned.
The education, the wife and family, all they had earned.
For some life would never be okay again,
Destroyed minds and bodies from the hell where they'd been.
That's the price that's paid for the effects of war.
When will we learn and say "no more."
Yet there are times when there's no other way.
That's when the common man has his say.
Most vets would deny that they were so great.

They just did great things. It was their fate.

4. Boot Camp
Dear Mom and Dad,
You won't believe all I've been through the last few days.
They got all of us enlistees together, and we left with no
delays.
The bus took us to the train station in Milwaukee.
We made a few stops and wound up at Parris Island, S.C.
They assigned us barracks, and we met our DI.
That's for drill instructor. He's going to make us all die.
It seems we must run everywhere we go down here.
I sweat so much I'm glad it's this time of year.
We went through this warehouse and got uniforms, all new.
They said we need nothing else. Our civies will be sent to you.
We do physical training (or PT to us Gyrenes).
It's worse than football practice when we were teens
You know what the DI said? He's as mean as can be.
"Your soul belongs to Jesus, but your ass belongs to me."
Sorry, Mom, but there is a lot of swearing here.
I'll try to remember not to around those I hold dear.
We all got physical exams. I won't say what they check.
I'm okay, but a couple of guys failed. They said what the heck.
Some have all the luck, just a little joke there.
We went to the barber. Now no one has any hair.
We ran obstacle courses, and the DI cursed us out.
He calls us damn Yankees and slime balls, always with a
shout.
He says he's going to make us Marines or we'll die trying.
I won't ever do it, but sometimes I feel like crying.
The other guys are like me. We won't ever stop.
We won't be what that DI calls us, pig slop.
I better go since we have inspection soon.
They check everybody and everything in the whole platoon.
I love you guys. However, I hate my DI.

Please say a prayer for me. Semper Fi.
That's how us Marines say goodbye.

Your loving son,
Clem

5. Wake Island

"Major, we have a radio message. It's coded, sir."
"What's going on that requires code? Are you sure?"
"Here's the code book. Give me a sec.
Good God. The Japs have attacked. Let me check.
Pearl Harbor's been bombed. Ships have been sunk."
"Sound the alarm. Tell everyone it's not bunk."
Wake Island is in the middle of the vast Pacific.
It had recently been armed, with Marines to be specific.
They mounted six of the five inch artillery guns.
Plus a dozen three inch, the antiaircraft type ones.
There were over a thousand civilians working there.
They were building a base due to the war scare.
"I hear aircraft coming in from the west.
They're bombers. I can see the rising sun crest.
Take cover. Take cover. Man those guns.
They're going to blast us with their bomb runs."
The damage was light, but of 12 aircraft on the ground,
Only four were left flyable, they later found.
The casualties were few. Some buildings were flat.
This was the first round. They were aware of that.
Japanese ships arrived four days later.
The Marines were ready. Now their response would be
    greater.
"Hold your fire until they're within range.
Don't tip them off. We'll be ready for an exchange.."
The remaining four aircraft, Marine Wildcats they were.
They took off with those Jap ships being the spur.
One destroyer was sunk, a Wildcat bomb sealed its doom.
Shore fire got a second. For all hands both were a tomb.

5

The "Hayate" was the first Jap ship sunk in the war.
The flag ship cruiser was almost one more.
With these loses the Japs called it a day,
But they'd be back for another foray.
Two carriers joined them from the Pearl Harbor force.
On Dec. 23 the second Wake Island invasion took its course.
This time the defenders were overwhelmed by the Jap attack.
We shot down 21 aircraft and sank two patrol boats fighting
     back.
Not counting sailors, the Japs lost 850 men.
We lost 130, but over 1500 POWs were taken.
The commander had sought resupply during the
     fighting lapse.
He finished his list with, "Send more Japs."
Unfortunately, there was no resupply at Wake.
But, "Be careful what you wish for, for the men's
     sake."

6. Hammerin Hank
Back in '27, Henry Elrod joined the Marines.
This seemed a logical choice from back in his teens.
He was chosen for Officer Candidate School.
Since he was a kid, he thought flying was cool.
Naval Flight School was the path he later chose.
He graduated, and over the years his rank rose.
On Dec. 4 of '41 Captain Elrod arrived for Wake Island's
     defense.
With the First Marine Defense Battalion because times were
     tense.
They weren't ready for the Dec. 7 bomber attack on Wake.
None of the 12 planes got airborne. What a bad break.
"Captain, they really junked our planes, but four look okay.
They have light damage. The men can get them fixed in a
     day."

"Have them load up with general purpose bombs.
The Jap navy will be next. I hope the weather stays calm."
Captain Elrod was right, and the Japs had no air.
The Wildcats took off, but they waited up there.
Their sign was the shore batteries' firing.
They dove at the ships, a sight most inspiring.
Captain Elrod got a hit, either by luck or by skill.
The "Kisaragi's" depth charge store exploded and all were
     killed.
Later during a second air attack, Henry did what heroes do,
He flew into a flight of 22 Jap Zeros and downed two.
Captain Elrod was killed while defending Wake on the
     ground.
No longer flying but where there's action, there he was found.
"Hammerin Hank" earned the first pilot's Medal of Honor of
     the war.
Buried in Arlington National Cemetery, a great example of
     military lore.

7. Wake Afterward

Over 400 military and 1100 civilians became POWs of Japan.
Moving them elsewhere for slave labor was their plan.
However, they kept 98 civilians for work there.
Later in '43 the Japs became well aware,
That we were invading other Pacific isles.
Maybe they worried about later war crime trials.
Their commander ordered that all POWs be shot.
They were machine gunned on the spot.
One lone man escaped. No one knows his name.
He left a message that recorded the shame.
98 USPW 5-10-43 carved on a coral stone.
Left there so the mass grave site would be known.
This last man was captured with nowhere to hide.
The Jap commander made sure that he died.
He personally beheaded him with his sword

Figuring that no one would ever say a word.
However, other officers wrote of atrocities after the war.
For the commander the punishment didn't even the score.
He was hung. It should have been more.
The grave site was found with the help of the stone mark.
The unknown POWs were reburied in Honolulu Memorial
    Park.

8. Bataan
For the Japs December 7 was an active day.
They bombed the Philippines, and it became their prey.
Small advanced parties landed here and there.
They were gathering intel, the invasion to prepare.
On December 22 at Lingayen Gulf, they came.
The main island of Luzon was their aim.
The defenders were organized in U.S. Army groups,
Which were composed mostly of Filipino troops.
We fell back. It was called a fighting retreat.
Our forces combined, on Bataan we'd meet.
This was a peninsula with no exit but the sea.
The Japs gradually advanced. We had nowhere to flee.
The troops held out hope. We'll get support soon.
We'll get supplies. We'll get reinforcements, a boon.
The Navy's coming. They'll evacuate our men.
They didn't know how. They didn't know when.
But sadly enough, there was no help coming.
Our country had nothing. The thought was numbing.
They were in the jungle with disease and the heat.
They were starving with no ammunition and nowhere to
    retreat.
For three months 'til April 9th, the Japs were delayed.
An offer to surrender to them was relayed.
General MacArthur had said, "No surrender allowed."
He himself had evacuated. He certainly was unbowed.
"We are not barbarians," the Japanese commander said,

When our man, for the welfare of our troops pled.
Some of the Army rowed small boats to Corregidor.
There the resistance lasted only one month more.
80,000 men surrendered, 12,000 Americans included.
They didn't know what was in store. They were deluded.
What came was the worst for our troops in the war.
Maybe they would have died fighting had they known what
     was in store.

9. Death March

We surrendered, starving, no means of defense, sick.
The Japs rounded us up from the jungles thick.
The first order of business, they robbed everything.
Watches, money, all with value, even wedding rings.
Then the march of 61 miles began.
Not too bad with water and food if you're a healthy man.
But you see, none of this was true, thus the trial.
Some would find it hard to walk the first mile.
Our troops learned the orders from on high.
Fall out, you die. Collapse and don't get up, you die.
Complain of the treatment or help a friend,
Both actions asked for a bloody end.
The Jap guards used the bayonet in the gut.
Maybe the prisoner would bleed out fast from the cut.
This was better than being run over by a truck in the rear.
Toward the fallen, the drivers would purposely steer.
The poor Filipino peasants tried to do a good deed.
They were shot for giving water to those in need.
One atrocity was especially abhorred, here's why.
Mounted soldiers would behead men as they drove by.
Damn little water, damn little food, no medical care,
It's surprising that so many made it there.
By railroad car the prisoners finished their trip.
They were interned at Camp O'Donnell, more hardship.
Of the 80,000 prisoners, 21,000 died on the way.

Thus,"Death March" is how we remember those days.
Some would excuse the Japs since we were disgraced.
Surrender was the reason for the cruelty we faced.
The Japs knew the Geneva Convention set of rules,
And those who accept their behavior are worse than fools.
Postscript
The POWs were shipped out for slave labor to various lands.
These were Formosa and China and back to Japan.
The Shinyo Maro was torpedoed by a US sub in '44.
688 POW's were killed in this military error.
Of all calamities these men needed no more.

10. No Forgiveness

"We've been walking and walking ever so long.
I can't make any mistakes. I can't do anything wrong.
My buddy Jim, a great guy but sort of a nut,
Just begged for some water and got it in the gut.
Military men march. We can't even walk.
We struggle and straggle. We can't even talk.
Concentrate on your balance. You must never fall.
No one can help you. They won't even let you crawl.
So many things can result in your death.
I must keep going to my very last breath.
The thousand mile journey begins with one step,
Then another and another until there's nothing left.
The guards seem to enjoy killing a helpless man.
What kind of people are these from Japan?
Should I follow the dictates from my Church?
Should I pray for them as I stumble and lurch?
I must forgive them to save my own soul.
But not today. Not 'til I'm ready for my personal hole.
In the mean time my own feeling is nothing but hate.
These little men should suffer with a slow death their fate.
I'll forgive when I'm ready, even if it is too late."

11. Japanese "Attacks" on the USA

After Pearl Harbor people were nervous, especially in the
     west.
No one knew, would the Japs continue their quest?
We seemed defenseless. They had sunk or damaged our ships.
Would their carriers come close and give us the slip?
What would be next, San Francisco, San Diego, or LA?
False alarms were widespread. We seems easy prey.
But the Jap fleet sailed west after the Pearl Harbor attack.
Instead several submarines patrolled, a Jap wolf pack.
They sunk some ten ships along California's coast,
And shelled an oil field and a military post.
The shelling ruined a pump and a baseball backstop,
But more seriously, a phone cable was chopped.
Later a submarine launched a seaplane twice.
Their fire bombs damaged nothing. Scaring us would suffice.
All damage was minor by any way you judge,
But the effect was, they gave our nervousness a nudge.
In '45 the Japs sent 9000 fire balloons in from the sea.
Six people died from their windblown spree.
These were the only casualties on the mainland USA,
From Jap attack attempts in all the war days.

Chapter 2.   On the Attack, 1942

1. The Doolittle Raid

The country was worried. We were under attack.
To build our morale we should be fighting back.
The President wanted the military to come up with a plan.
Two weeks after Pearl Harbor the process began.
Someone suggested an air attack on Japan from the sea.
With planes heavier than the Navy's like the Army's B-25B.
They painted lines on a runway, a carrier's length.
Yes, the B-25 could take off. It had enough strength.
However, it was too heavy to make a landing.
For Naval planes requirements are more demanding.
With a 2000 pound load and 2400 mile range, the B-25
Could get its crew over Japan and back over land alive.
Russia refused help. With Japan they weren't at war.
So China was it. We could reach her shore.
They cut the plane's weight, no self defense.
Reducing the crew to five made a lot of sense.
Col. Jimmy Doolittle was leader for the foray.
By damn, he hoped he'd get them home okay.
On April 18 of '42 the carrier Hornet was ready.
They sailed into the wind. The ship was steady.
Sixteen planes prepared for their takeoff.
Leaving the flight deck they dropped, then climbed aloft.
The Hornet was not far enough from Japan's coast.
So they turned tail, and to the Japs became a ghost.
The B-25s bombed Tokyo and other cities.
Little damage was done, so no need for pity.
One plane flew to Russia, the crew interned for a year.
The remainder crashed in China, the crews jumping clear.
Eleven men didn't make it back to our side,
Though they completed their history making ride.

Of these the Japs executed three,
While four died later in captivity.
The Japs were so incensed, their homeland was at risk,
They punished the Chinese and 250,000 perished.
These peasants may have helped our men escape.
This was the excuse for extermination and rape.
What did we gain from our daring attack?
A propaganda victory and a the warning,"We'll be back."

2. The Battle of the Coral Sea

The Japs continued their conquest of the Pacific isles.
Dutch East Indies fell and this covered a million square miles.
Mostly there was little or no resistance to their attack.
There wasn't much we could do while falling back.
We had one advantage, we could break their code.
This intel would help. Their advance could be slowed.
They had a task force with an invasion plan.
Port Moresby in New Guinea was where they'd land.
For later attacks on Australia, they'd have bases there.
They also chose to invade Tulagi, an island near.
The Coral Sea is northeast of Australia by 500 miles.
Most of the action happened there and around nearby isles.
The battle took place from May 4 to 8 in '42.
This was the first time in history where naval tactics were so
    new.
No ship fired on another or even was seen.
All the action was with aircraft flying between.
There were two carriers plus support ships in each fleet.
Strangely, none of these ships would meet.
Planes from the Yorktown struck the Japs first.
They damaged several ships, but for the Japs that's not the
    worst.
They stopped Japan's Port Moresby invasion, what's more
Japan was never able to invade there during the war.
However, the Japs became aware of our presence there,

On the seventh the major battle was sea-air.
Tactically, with one of our carriers lost the Japs won.
The Lexington had to be scuttled. She was done.
The severely damaged Yorktown was under tow,
With no power she'd received a serious blow.
However, we had achieved a strategic victory in the Coral Sea.
Due to damage and lack of planes the Japs had to flee.
Neither carrier was available for the Midway fight.
And to our ally Australia, chances looked more bright.

3. What a Lady

The Yorktown was towed across the sea.
For thousands of miles to Hawaii she had to flee.
The sailors started work to fix their ship.
In Honolulu the repair crews worked at a fast clip.
To make her seaworthy, they had three days,
And to get rearmed, restocked, refueled and underway.
Her engines were in working order, her elevators too.
They set sail again with an expanded crew.
The civilian workers were still on board.
They got everything working with a prayer to the Lord.
The Yorktown got to Midway for the next fight,
One month after Coral Sea, and all was right.
She was attacked again, the Japs had another go.
The gallant Yorktown again was in tow.
But this time a Jap sub lurking nearby,
Torpedoed our warship, and this time she died.
Our tough old carrier slipped beneath the wave.
What a lady, we salute you in your grave.
You're a testament to our country, the land of the brave.

4. The Code Trick

After the Coral Sea battle in May of '42,
Something else was coming, the American Command knew.
The Jap navy with their carriers would attack, but where.

A plan was hatched by a code breaker there.
Now when they say breaking code, it's not complete.
They get bits and pieces. It's never really neat.
There's inferences, and probabilities, and guess work,
By men who study messages. They're code breaking clerks.
The Japs' radio message referred to "AF" they knew.
For the location of their target, this was a clue.
Commander Rochefort sent a message in the clear.
This was from Midway, "We have a water shortage here."
A later Jap message made a reference in code.
They reported the "AF" water problem episode.
This fixed the place of the attack, not when.
However, it allowed intelligent deployment of ships and men.

5. Midway Preparations

Midway is not a single island but an atoll.
The two largest islands played a military roll.
On Eastern Island an airfield pretty much filled the place.
Sand Island had the remainder of the military base.
The atoll is the most northwest of the Hawaiian chain.
It's 1300 miles from Honolulu, and I must explain.
Halfway across the Big Pond is where Midway lies.
That's equidistant between California and China as the crow
     flies.
After Pearl Harbor the effort was made
To provide for the island's defense upgrade.
After the code breakers found out Japan's invasion plan,
The addition of antiaircraft guns and planes began.
There's always the unforeseen, it happens in every war.
The Navy decided to plant demolition charges, an error.
By accident the men managed to blow up the fuel dump.
This destroyed the tanks, the piping, and the pumps.
One Marine officer made a comment, not a spoof.
"You can make it fool, but not sailor proof."
The Marines had their aircraft stationed on the base.

Fighters, dive bombers, and torpedo planes filled the space.
Of large bombers they decided they needed more.
Four B-26 and 19 B-17s came from the Army Air Corps.
The Navy brought 32 PBY Catalina scout planes
Altogether on the fuel supply, this caused strains.
Fuel was brought in hundreds of steel drums.
Still the airmen were limited to few practice runs.
This fuel dump fiasco certainly was not a good start
For the big fight in which all would take part.

6. Marine Air

The U. S. Marines flew Naval aircraft in the war.
However, they were the last to get updated hardware.
On Midway they had the F2A, the Buffalo by name.
These were called "Brewsters" and because of their fame.
"Flying Coffins" was how they were better known.
One captain said, "Any commander who orders them flown
Should consider the pilot lost before he leaves the ground."
When they flew against the Jap Zero, they were so found.
The dive bombers were the SB2U Vindicators.
These were known as "Vibrators or Wind Indicators."
The Marines did have six F4F Wildcat fighters there
And six torpedo bombers, TBF Avengers. Both were fair.
The Jap fleet was detected early on June fourth.
We attacked them for all we were worth.
The Marine dive bombers and torpedo planes had a go.
The Army Marauders and Flying Fortresses joined the show.
Even the lumbering Catalinas were fitted out
With torpedoes to add to their clout.
In the meantime the Japs attacked Midway from the air.
All our aircraft were aloft when they got there.
The results of these fights were disastrous to our side.
We suffered mostly from the Zero, the Japanese pride.
This nimble fast fighter caused most of our loss.
Having inferior equipment, we had to bear the cross.

With our sacrifice, what did we gain?
Against the Jap carrier fleet, the results were plain.
No hits due to bombs from either dive or level flight,
Our torpedoes missed or failed outright.
However, the Jap attack on the Midway Isles
Was not particularly effective, and we survived that trial.
We did down some Jap planes in the attacking force,
And we learned things that helped in the war's course.
1. At high altitude the Zeroes were outrun by the Flying Fort.
2. Don't send bombers with no fighter escorts.
3. The Catalina is good for rescuing pilots at sea.
4. Get new torpedoes and fighters as fast as can be.
The men on Midway thought they were alone.
They didn't know if or when our Navy would come along.

7. Interception
Our Midway radars were of the latest design.
They detected the incoming Japanese air with plenty of time.
Our fighters took off to challenge the attack.
Soon they realized the Zeroes were on their backs.
"Go for those clouds off on the right.
There's no way this will be an even fight."
"I can feel the slugs hitting the back of my seat."
This was armored. Thank God for that steel sheet.
His head was not covered, so he pulled it down.
"I'm heading for the deck. I'd rather drown."
The Jap pilot was skilled but wouldn't dare
Come too close to the water down there
He pulled out of the dive with the Zero behind.
"I'm going to pull a sudden stop, the stall kind."
He cut the power and deployed his dive brakes.
The Zero shot forward. This was a new fake.
He lifted his nose and let out a gun blast.
The Zero received the death blow as he flew past.
Our fighters couldn't compare with the Zero's speed,

But we had two advantages, all the crews agreed.
There was some armor to protect the pilot's skin,
And the fuel tanks were self-sealing keeping the gas in.
After the fracas, they landed, those few surviving soles.
In one plane there were over 200 bullet holes.
Some survived and ditched at sea.
They were picked up by the PBYs or the sleek PT.
Meanwhile on the ground the antiaircraft crews
Blasted away at the raiders who paid their dues.
Showing his scorn one Jap pilot flew over upside down.
The Marine gunner paused looking at this crazy clown.
Then he blasted him as he flew by.
One more Zero blown out of the sky.
The Japs paid for their attack on our shore
Unfortunately for our side, we paid more.
However, the Japs felt another raid was in store.

8. The Battle

What a way to spend a beautiful June day.
All the attacks on the Jap fleet didn't pay.
The Marine and Air Corps flew from Midway's field.
Now maybe the Naval carrier planes would provide a yield.
They first sent their torpedo planes in low.
It turned out just as bad. They received a blow.
Ninety percent of all torpedo planes didn't make it back.
Maybe the dive bombers would do better in their attack.
Now unbeknown to us, the Japs planned a second wave.
They wanted to bomb Midway into the grave.
General purpose bombs were mounted on their planes.
Then they heard our carriers were sighted, a change was
        ordained.
Rearm all the planes with torpedoes to attack our ships.
There was no time to store ordinance, a real slip.
The ideal time to attack a carrier and cause a wreck
Is when their planes are armed and lined up on deck.

The Japanese fleet had four carriers sailing there.
Our dive bombers plummeted down out of the air.
No Zeroes met them, their carriers to save.
They had spent their time chasing the last attacking wave.
Bombs hit three flight decks and penetrated through.
They had delay fuses. Time passed before they blew.
The bombs detonated on the hangar decks below.
Amongst gas lines, bombs, and planes ready to go..
Three infernos were created by our attack.
None of these ships would ever fight back.
The fourth carrier was not hit by bombs at all.
It launched its own planes to continue the brawl.
The gallant Yorktown was better prepared when they arrived.
The Japs hit it with torpedo planes and those that dived
Our carrier was knocked out but not for long.
The sailors made temporary fixes. Our lady was strong.
Hours later the Yorktown was attacked again.
This time she was not so fortunate as she had been.
The captain decided that they should abandon ship.
The Yorktown was dying. Soon beneath the waves she'd slip.
We retaliated and dive bombed the last Jap carrier
Even though there was a strong Zero barrier.
There was minor action for the next two days.
We sank a Jap cruiser along the way.
Comparing loses, the important point was our gain.
They lost four carriers with all their planes.
Our Yorktown, a destroyer, and 130 planes were lost.
Over 3000 Jap sailors and 300 of ours was the human cost.
The Battle of Midway ended on the seventh of June.
Six months since the "Day of Infamy," none too soon.
This was the battle that changed the course of the Pacific war.
We went on the offensive. We'd even the score.

9. Lost at Sea
They'd dropped their torpedo, then flew toward the sun.

A few shells had hit them on their run.
"Sir, I'm wounded on my upper arm.
I can still move it, so not too much harm."
"Try to stop the bleeding. Did you feel that jerk?
The engine's sputtering. Maybe I can make it work."
The Avenger lost altitude. They were going down.
If they made a crash landing, they'd surely drown.
"I'm going to try to keep the nose up high.
I'll catch a wave just right if I try."
The plane hit the water, and quickly it slowed.
They opened the canopy and got stuff that was stowed.
There were rations, water, and an inflatable raft.
With the parachutes, they'd test their survival craft.
They evacuated the plane, and then it sank.
Prayers were said, to God they said thanks.
The parachutes were handy for awning and sail,
And collecting rain water or to avoid the need to bail.
How many days at sea? Too hard to tell.
Our pilot scratched his arm each morn, or forgot, oh well.
Their rations were gone. What could they do?
An albatross was caught, very tough to chew.
They thought of the Ancient Mariner and his curse.
Would killing the bird make their predicament worse?
"Sir, there's a submarine coming our way.
Oh crap, it's Japanese. Will they treat us okay?"
No need to worry. The Japs looked and passed by.
Two lost Americans weren't worth bothering with, is why.
"Dear Lord, if we should survive this ordeal,
Let me remember one thought. It's how I feel.
For 500 miles with no man made light,
The vast star filled sky, it's truly an awesome sight."
The pilot, 24, and his gunner, 19, were rescued by a PBY.
They'd spent 17 days. It wasn't their time to die.
They would recover though each had lost 60 pounds.
The resilience of youth knows few bounds.

10. Bailout

If you were shot down and went into the sea,
You stood a better chance being as far as can be
From the air action that could cause your demise.
The Jap Zeroes liked to pull a surprise.
Whether in the water or dangling from ropes,
They used you for target practice. You had little hope.
However, a crew of two was picked up near by.
The Japs interrogated them, information to ply.
When they were done, the Jap commander, what a gem,
Said any sailor would get a watch who would execute them.
All his sailors refused, so he had an alternate plan.
They tied weights on the legs of each man.
And tossed them overboard. They were still alive.
It was a quick death, no way to survive.

11. Dear Mom and Dad,

Well, we've been at sea for a week now.
We're on this old ship. I'd call it a scow.
Before coming on board, we did a lot of practice landing.
I can't tell you where that was. It was quite demanding.
In a letter they won't let you say too much,
Where we were, where we're going, the ship's name and such.
Actually, no one knew where we were going to.
Then a few days ago, the news came through.
All I can say is, it's really humid and hot.
Makes me miss all the snow and ice we've got.
I spend a lot of time topside especially at night.
Where my bunk is below, it's like an oven. It stinks outright.
I'm doing okay, and the chow's pretty good,
But I'd sure like more fresh types of food.
The others like to complain about the chow.
Marines do that a lot somehow.
We had a church service Sunday last.

I figured you'd like to hear that. Are you aghast?
Oh, there's one thing that gets me here,
No showers, no shaving, since water's too dear.
The guys like to gamble and play cards a lot.
That's not for me. I like to keep what I've got.
We chew the fat and pass on the scuttlebutt.
That's military jingo for rumor of which there's a glut.
My buddies like to brag what they'll do to the Japs.
I won't tell you the details. Sometimes they're saps.
How are the kids? Is Orville still in school?
Tell him to finish and not be a fool.
If he wants to join the Marines, don't sign for him.
He can wait 'til he's eighteen, and not join on a whim.
Coming up we have some practice drill.
I have to clean my weapons again. I've had my fill.
I love you guys. Tell everyone I miss them.
Semper Fi.

Your loving son,
Clem.

12. Landing on Guadalcanal

Japan had conquered the most western Pacific isles.
In the south they wanted to expand control by many miles.
This was for bases for future Australian raids.
Or to provide interdiction of our supply convoys by blockade.
In early '42 they invaded several islands including
    Guadalcanal.
This jungle covered spot had the right locale
For building an airfield. This fit the overall plan
Of creating a large area controlled by Japan.
Guadalcanal is part of the Solomon Island chain.
The need for regaining control was plain.
It is a fairly large island, 30 by 90 miles about.
Early in the war our ability to invade was in doubt.
The landing was on August seventh of 1942.

We were on the offensive. Some said it was past due.
With thickening clouds the convoy could proceed.
The Japs wouldn't detect them it was agreed.
The transports were slow and defenseless, sitting ducks.
If nature cooperated, they'd be in luck.
The cruisers bombarded inland as well as the shore.
This softening up was necessary with this type war.
If you can blast apart some enemy fortifications,
You reduce the invading Marines tribulations.
The troops climbed aboard the small landing craft.
They could get closer to land with their shallow draft.
"Why aren't they shooting? We're certainly in reach."
"Maybe they'll get us when we hit the beach."
But they landed with no resistance from the Japs.
The Marines moved inland always expecting traps.
They set up a defense. Supplies were brought ashore.
Everything was limited. They could use more.
With their objective the Jap airfield, the Marines moved out.
The enemy was nowhere with none to rout.
They found all types of supplies everywhere.
The Jap defenders had left it all right there.
This was fortunate since the Navy pulled back.
Even though of food and ammo there was a lack.
At that time we definitely did not have control of the sea.
We had to safeguard our ships all agreed.
The 11,000 Marines formed a defensive perimeter at first.
On scrounging and making do, they were well versed.
Jap equipment, Jap tents, even Jap food they used.
I'm sure the Jap military wouldn't be amused.
Even then the Marines had only two meals a day.
They had just ten days worth of ammo to their dismay.
They finished the airfield, Henderson Field it was named.
After a heroic Marine aviator. At Midway he earned his fame.
Two weeks after the invasion, aircraft landed there.
This gave our troops a chance in the future hell they shared.

13. Tulagi

Several islands near Guadalcanal were occupied by the Japs.
A seaplane base on Tulagi Island filled in their patrol gaps.
On August seventh 3000 Marines landed there.
Like Guadalcanal the invasion went with little care.
The pre-invasion bombardment caused the enemy to flee.
They had prepared positions, caves in from the sea.
As many as 40 Jap naval troops occupied each of these.
With a narrow opening they wouldn't be taken with ease.
The Marines threw in grenades. These were thrown back.
They tried out another technique in their attack.
Usually, officers would command in the following way,
"Sargent, take a squad and do as I say."
This was not for Captain T. He picked four men.
They covered him as he charged a cave like den.
He lit the fuze on a bundle of dynamite sticks and tossed it
    inside.
This did the trick. Most of the Japs died.
Captain T repeated this procedure 50 times more*.
Once he added a five gallon gas tank to even the score.
That time he miscalculated and blew off his own pants.
"Boy that was a real pisser," he commented after taking that
    chance.
Captain T lead a charmed life with only one bullet in the butt.
His wrist watch was shot off, lucky though a nut.
We liberated those islands in just three days.
However, 122 Marines paid in this war byway.
*A slight exaggeration I expect.
We'll never know just what's correct.

14. The Battle of Savo Island

The Marines had landed on Guadalcanal Isle.
Jap aircraft showed up to attack in a short while.
All the supplies had not been moved ashore.

Transport ships got underway. They knew the score.
The Japs went for them avoiding the warships nearby.
They wanted to interfere with the invasion is why.
Carrier planes showed up and engaged the Japs.
Antiaircraft guns on the warships joined the scrap.
Unfortunately, the "Eliott" was bombed and caught fire.
All the men on board escaped the destruction most dire.
The second night the Japs sent a battle fleet
To do their part, the landing force to defeat.
One approach to Guadalcanal was known as "The Slot."
The Japs sailed this channel to take their shot.
Their presence had been noted by sub and by air.
Our own ships went to Savo Island and met them there.
Unknown to us, the Japs had practiced at night.
None knew of this tactic for naval fight.
Their flares and searchlights were effectively used,
And our Navy was certainly abused.
We suffered three ships damaged and four cruisers sunk.
The Japs sustained only damage but away they slunk.
It seems they were afraid of daylight and our planes,
So they turned back in spite of their gains.
Main result: this battle was the reason our ships went to sea,
Leaving the Marines alone to a large degree.
They toughed it out. Marines are the best you'll agree.

15. Dear Mom and Dad(2),

Quite a bit has happened since I last wrote.
I'm not sure what I can say of note.
We didn't have to fight the Japs for awhile.
They must have fled to the far end of the isle.
Now they're giving up. They're starving and sick.
Most were construction workers. It's not a trick.
We got enough exercise when we first came ashore
By carrying supplies to where they were stored.
A truck or two would certainly have helped here.

They couldn't get any ashore cause of the air raid fear.
Jap bombers make frequent raids on the airfield.
They rarely damage anything. Not much of a yield.
Then we got the Marine Air stationed on our base.
They now meet those bombers and give them chase.
We've had a few shellings from Japanese ships.
They only show up at night, giving our planes the slip.
I've heard we have a sub visit nearly every night.
He's called "Oscar." He's an observer and doesn't want to
    fight.
We Marines had some action, call it a jungle war.
It's a rotten place to fight. I'd like no more.
The Japs hide up in the palms and wait to attack
'Til after we pass. They fire to hit us in the back.
They can only do this once to the unaware.
Every Marine responds with bullets through their lair.
We decided this is stupid as well as being wrong.
They certainly raise our ire, and they don't live long.
I'm going on patrol, and I have to get some chow.
Keep writing. I haven't gotten any letters up to now
Sarge says the mail will come through any day.
I know he's right. In wartime that's the way.
How are the dogs? I miss you and them.
Semper Fi

Your loving son,
Clem.

16. The Long Battle
The Japs had a hard job landing supplies and troops.
They wanted to move in, unload, and then scoot.
We couldn't attack them during nighttime hours.
In daytime they should be out of range of those planes of ours.
They settled on destroyers, not much cargo, but fast.
They could carry men, but their supplies wouldn't last.
Our Marines called this supply system the "Tokyo Express."

The Japs, mostly naval troops, though tough were under
    duress.
The tide of war would ebb and flow.
Neither could drive the other out whatever the blow.
Each time the Japs tried transports during the day.
Marine and later Army Air would blow them away.
The Marines had been there longer of course.
They called themselves the CAF or "Cactus Air Force."
The Jap aircraft had an 1100 mile round trip.
Leaving not much time to find and attack our ships.
The Jap navy tried to blast Henderson Field at night.
Their most successful try was with battleship might.
Our airbase was destroyed with all the plane fuel.
We were back in operation a day after that duel.
Both sides suffered from the jungle war.
Dysentery and malaria somewhat evened the score.
Finally, after about six months of this war of attrition,
The Japs evacuated those they could with a rescue mission.
They lost over 30,000 to our 7000 men.
Their 38 ship loss exceeded ours by ten.
Aircraft loss was one third more than the 600 of ours.
For Japan this was more severe, a loss of power.
We could replace our losses. For them it was too big a chore.
The battle of Guadalcanal was a turning point of the war.
We pushed the Japs out with the promise of more.

From an unknown Marine:
When our man gets to heaven, to St. Peter he will tell,
"One more Marine reporting, Sir. I've spent my time in hell."

17. Dear Mr. And Mrs. Hanson,

You probably know what this letter is for.
Clem died last week, a casualty of the war.
I was Clem's platoon leader here on Guadalcanal.
We are not allowed to fraternize, but he was my pal.

I want you to know he was always a good guy.
It seems so unfair that the best should die.
I want you to know how the situation was here.
The Japs threw everything at us with not a care.
It was the Battle of Lunga Ridge if it makes the news.
Clem was killed protecting two wounded of his crew.
He was a hero. Please understand this fact.
He never faltered. This is how he would act.
If I survive this war with the Japs some day,
I plan to come visit you if I may.
Please say a prayer for us who have survived so far.
Semper Fi

> God be with you,
> Lt. John Wilbar.

18. The Fighting Sullivans

Genevieve's boy friend was killed in the Pearl Harbor attack.
Her five brothers wanted to pay the bastards back.
As a group they enlisted in January of '42.
They were from Iowa, the small town of Waterloo.
The Navy had a policy of separating siblings then,
Though this was not strictly enforced for all men.
They were assigned to the Juneau, a light cruiser.
She participated in several battles, she wasn't a loser.
She took a torpedo at Iron Bottom Sound.
This area near Guadalcanal saw many ships downed.
The Juneau and several others left the area for repair.
She took another torpedo from a Jap sub lurking there.
The Juneau's magazine exploded and under she slipped.
To those nearby it seemed none survived the sinking ship.
Now the rest of the story, about which most are unaware.
The other damaged ships saw no reason to search there.
All were afraid they would take a torpedo too.
They did notify a patrolling B-17 about possible surviving
        crew.

The aircraft wouldn't break radio silence while in the air.
They finished their patrol, then wrote a report with care.
Unfortunately, the report got buried for several days.
When it was found, search planes flew without delay.
The surviving crew were found eight days after the sinking, by
    a PBY.
Of the hundred who left the Juneau only ten didn't die.
These survived the hunger, shark attacks and thirst.
Three Sullivans died on the ship, but what was worse,
One drowned a day later, and the last lost his mind.
He swam away from the raft, maybe his brothers to find.
That's how the Fighting Sullivans lost their lives at sea.
If there were no screw ups, maybe the dead would be but
    three.
To make matters worse, to keep secrets from the Japs,
News of a ship sinking was kept under wraps.
The Sullivan parents were told three months after the fact.
Somehow, they knew when letters stopped coming back.
There was one good result, the rules for brothers became a
    pact.

19. The Knock

"What's the matter dear, you've been kind of blue?"
"Well, we haven't gotten any letters like we usually do.
Ah hell, there's the door. I'll be late for work."
He could see three men in the early morning murk.
With two officers and an enlisted man, Tom Sullivan was
    stunned.
Holding back his grief, all he could say was, "Which one?"
The ranking officer gulped and then revived.
"I'm really sorry sir, but it's all five."
How do you soften a blow such as this?
The answer is, you can't. It's a duty you'd rather miss.
Suddenly their boys are all gone, lost at sea.
The family can't even say goodbye as it should be.

No wake, no funeral, no burial plot.
The memories of their boy hoods is all they've got.
Dear Lord, is there anything we can do except pray
That the world's leaders learn not to stray?
No parent wants his sons to die this way.

Chapter 3.   European Theater, 1942, 1943

1. The Coast Guard
The Coast Guard always had jobs off our shore.
They tried to stop smugglers. They rescued shipwrecked and
more.
Even before our entry into World War II,
Their duties were expanded by adding a few.
They reported weather especially off Greenland's coast.
This and iceberg spotting were important for our shipping
host.
They became convoy escorts when the war started
Twelve German subs were sunk, others were thwarted.
The cutter Campbell rammed a U-boat which quickly sank.
Their dog mascot Sinbad became a hero of enlisted rank.
Even though in convoys, too often ships went down.
The Coast Guard cutters limited the men who drowned.
The troopship Dorchester's sinking became well known.
The Coast Guard rescued many acting on their own.
In addition their coxswains crewed many landing craft.
These were the Higgins boats and others of shallow draft.
They were in the North Africa and Sicily landings.
On D-Day the Coast Guard's contribution was outstanding.
Not only did they pilot boats to the shore,
But off the coast they rescued 400 or more.
Coast Guard personnel did their share in the war.

2. About U-boats
U-boat is our adaptation of "Unterseeboot."
We've always felt their "Kriegsmarine" were really brutes.
The Germans developed their subs in World War I,
Diesel engines, electric power drive, the deck gun,

31

Pressure hulls, ballast systems, and safer fuel,
Contact, acoustic, or magnetic torpedoes most cruel.
Later in '44 they developed the snorkel device.
With this they could get enough air to suffice,
For running the diesel while submerged a bit,
And not be seen or by a shell get hit.
By resupply at sea, they extended their range
With special ships called "milk cows," how strange.
Their primary targets were their enemy's merchant fleet.
If you limited their supplies, it would hasten defeat.
The Germans often grouped U-boats, called a wolf pack.
This would result in more ships sunk in their attack.
The German surface navy was much too small then,
And their U-boats tended to make things more even.

3. The Battle of the Atlantic

Soon after the Pearl Harbor attack, Germany declared war on
    us.
Their deployment of U-boats resulted from the new status.
They took up station along the Atlantic coast.
Also, the Gulf of Mexico and Caribbean were their post.
Germany had been after British ships since '39,
When their war started. Now it was our time.
After a few months we had lost 350 ships
With over 50 sunk making the cross Gulf trips.
Mostly, we needed tankers to carry oil to the east.
Our rail system didn't have the capacity in the least.
The government made a set of rules for the night.
Blackouts of the coastal cities would lower background light.
The U-boats used silhouettes to see passing ships
Then they'd blast them and beneath the waves they'd slip.
The Coast Guard and Navy made many offshore runs,
But nothing seemed to still those U-boat guns.
With the U-boat surfaced most attacks were made.
There was no need to use torpedoes in the blockade.

It was known that armed convoys were the answer here.
The Navy objected but realized the necessity was clear.
The odds of a ship being sunk on a trip was one in ten.
This improved to one in 100 with the convoy system.
Of course, the U-boats also attacked ships crossing the sea.
Most of the Atlantic Navy's job was protecting these.
Still the Allies lost almost 3000 ships to them,
While 800 U-boats paid dearly for their stratagem.
One final note; we had the benefit of good intel.
Code breaking helped determine the U-boats' locations pretty
    well.
The men who manned these merchant ship crews,
Were all civilians. Like the military, they paid their dues.
They made their war contribution, but received little news.

4. Battle of the St. Lawrence

Big picture military actions often have a side that's light.
The U-boat menace hit home one dark night.
They attacked in the St. Lawrence river's wide mouth.
Mostly, we think that U-boats operated farther south.
They sank four ore carriers passing near,
And for good measure torpedoed the Bell Island pier.
Maybe this was the result of an accuracy lack.
The pier's damage wasn't so much of a whack,
But historically this was the only German North America
    attack.

5. Destroyer Attack

"Sir, I've got a hit, 30 degrees to port."
"What's your range?" This was not a sport.
"Coming up on 3000 yards. She's moving north."
"Battle stations, battle stations," the horn blasted forth.
The destroyers were protecting all ships afloat.
Their job was to find and destroy the enemy U-boat.
The convoy mostly consisted of freighter ships.

Through the destroyers' protective ring, U-boats shouldn't
    slip.
The convoy had been at sea now for ten days.
This was the first contact along the way.
"Coming up on 1000 yards. Estimated depth 100 feet."
"Steady as she goes. Hold onto your seat."
"We're coming up on her. She's diving Sir."
"Set depth charges for 300 feet. We'll scuttle her.
Fire every three seconds, starting...now, fire."
The depth charges or ash cans could cause results most dire.
The desired effect was they'd explode close enough
To cause a rupture in the pressure hull, quite tough.
For the U-boat crew this would be the very end.
There was no escape, to the bottom they'd descend.
Their only hope was damage less severe,
And they could surface and jump clear.
If they surrendered then, they'd be prisoners of war.
The U.S. Navy would spare them. That's the score.
The sonar man quickly ripped off his head phones.
The exploding depth charges would deafen, this was known.
Every three seconds the sailors felt the blasts.
All hoped they wouldn't have to make another pass.
After the last rumble, the sonar man listened and started
    thinking.
"I hear metal tearing. The U-boat seems to be sinking."
After a few minutes an oil slick appeared
This was a second sign about which the men cheered.
Another U-boat sent to her deep sea rest.
Nobody was concerned though they were amongst the best.
Over 28,000 Kriegsmarine died for the Nazi victory quest.

6. Four Chaplains
The Dorchester had sailed in mid winter of '43.
It was a small convoy that went to sea.
They took the northern route where it gets cold.

Maybe that's where the U-boats wouldn't be so bold.
The Dorchester was a troopship with 900 men.
They were 100 miles off the Greenland coast when
An explosion ripped amidships. They were done.
The four chaplains aboard rushed to the deck as one.
They thought they could calm the troops in their care.
They donned life jackets, then handed them elsewhere.
Then to everyone's dismay, the jackets ran out.
Each one of the chaplains removed his and turning about,
Gave them to the next four GIs they met.
In 18 minutes the troopship sank. Their deed we'll not forget.
The last anyone saw, the four were standing arm in arm.
Praying in their own ways that no GIs would come to harm.
Two Protestant ministers, a rabbi, and a priest,
Gave their lives to four boys among the very least.
Of the men on board and the Merchant Marine crew,
Only 230 were rescued by the cutters, there were two.
They disobeyed orders to chase the U-boat.
They rescued helpless men who couldn't stay afloat.
You don't last long submerged in Arctic water.
Maybe minutes before the hypothermal slaughter.
In the Naval history of World War II,
Only two other ships lost more passengers and crew.
They became known as the "Immortal Chaplains," these four.
For them Congress created a special "Medal of Valor."

7. Mark Clark
The French had surrendered early in the war.
Only the north of France was occupied, no more.
The Vichy government was allied with the Hun.
They ruled French North Africa since the Axis won.
In Morocco and Algeria, we planned to land our troops.
Would we be resisted by the French military groups?
A Polish spy ring reported the French would balk.
Eisenhower sent an envoy to clandestinely talk.

A British submarine surfaced off Algeria at night.
It carried a landing party. They saw a signal light.
Major General Mark Clark was paddled ashore.
He attended a planned meeting to find what was in store.
We spirited out one French general of high rank.
You'd think the British and Americans he'd thank.
Instead he demanded that he should lead the attack.
When his demand was rejected, he turned his back.
He decided to be "a spectator in this affair."
Even without his help, we expected little resistance there.
Our Navy had orders not to fire on the shore.
If the French fired first, then we could even the score.
For his daring escapade, Mark Clark got another star,
Becoming the youngest Lieutenant General by far.

8. Operation Torch

On Nov. 8 of '42 we landed on North Africa's shore
The invading forces were American, British and a few more.
The French Resistance made important contributions.
While the Vichy French tried to mess up the execution.
At Casablanca, French Morocco we landed our host,
Plus Oran and Algiers on the Algerian coast.
The western attackers traveled directly from the USA
With General Patton leading on the invasion day.
A coup d'etat had failed the night before.
This warned the Vichy commander what was in store.
Our ships didn't fire as we approached the beach,
But the coastal batteries opened up as we came within reach.
The French navy joined in the invasion fight.
Thirteen of their ships were sunk by our Navy's might.
We had two destroyers damaged in the fray,
While our troops were pinned on one beach for a day.
Fortunately we had air support from a carrier group.
They attacked coastal positions, ships and reinforcing troops.
The Casablanca battle was over in just three days.

Of the three invasion spots, this was the toughest foray.
The two other invasions started on the same day.
Their fleets traveled from Britain, a shorter way.
In Oran there was trouble with unexpected shallows.
The Vichy French opposition was hard to swallow.
Our attempt to land GIs directly on a pier
Was thwarted by crossfire from French vessels there.
The French navy broke from the harbor attacking us.
All were sunk or driven ashore, a big plus.
Heavy fire from a British battleship brought surrender on
     Nov. 9.
The French didn't fight to the death which is fine.
In Algiers the French resistance captured the local boss.
He wouldn't surrender no matter the French loss.
The Resistance silenced the defensive guns on the coast.
Which made it an easier landing there than most.
The Vichy French fired at ships trying to capture the port,
Driving them off. That plan they had to abort.
There were problems with this invasion along the way.
However, the Algiers commander surrendered later in the day.
The French reaction was strange to say the least.
Why did so many side with their historic enemy beast?
Whether common soldier or one of the officer class,
The Germans were occupying their country en masse.
We were trying to liberate them from this oppression.
You would think there'd be no need to get another lesson.

9. The Kasserine Pass

After the French surrendered in Africa's north,
We built up our forces so we could charge forth.
The Germans and Italians also built up their force.
They knew they would be fighting on two fronts in due
     course.
In North Africa the British had fought over two years.
From Egypt they had pushed the Afrika Korps near.

Both Allied armies would meet in Tunisia. Their goal
Was to push out the Axis and make them pay the toll.
The Allies had decoded a message, General Rommel's orders.
But Rommel didn't obey on how to defend their borders.
We were deployed in Western Tunisia in the wrong places.
Rommel, the Desert Fox, aimed at our supply bases.
The going was easy for us for awhile.
When the Axis panzers attacked, speed was their style.
First they tricked us by retreating to an ambush site.
Where their 88 artillery showed us their might.
Our tanks were blown apart, so we had to retreat.
You learn by your mistakes, more so when you're beat.
Orders were issued to defend a certain spot.
Artillery was ordered to fire with all they've got.
Typically, this was after the panzers passed by.
We didn't have any response. Men needlessly died.
In the Battle of the Kasserine Pass, you could say we lost.
We lost more equipment, especially tanks, and men. This was
    our cost.
But we kept our supply bases out of Rommel's reach.
And in six days the Axis had retreated from the breach.
After the battle many changes were made.
Ineffective officers were canned for not making the grade.
Better communication was ordered between the groups,
Especially for the artillery support of the ground troops.
It became the policy for the future of the war,
That commanders be close to the action, so they'd know
    more,
And leaders on the spot had more responsibility, the lesson's
    core.

10. Tunisia

Centered in North Africa, we wanted to set Tunisia free.
Strategically, it could control shipping in the Mediterranean
    Sea.

In early '43 the Axis found it harder and harder to supply
With the Allies gaining control of the neighboring sky.
The perimeter kept shrinking with the Brits on the east.
They had help from the Commonwealth nations at least.
The Americans with British and French units attacked from
    the west.
The Brits breached the Axis' Mareth defensive line in their
    quest.
Rommel knew it was over and suggested they leave.
Hitler would never countenance this, you better believe.
So Rommel was replaced by a more malleable man.
It didn't matter. Their fate was sealed whatever the plan.
On May 13 about six months after we had gone ashore,
The Axis surrendered. Of fighting, they wanted no more.
About 275,000 were captured and sent to the States.
Even then, more than this escaped the POW fate.
We treated them well in our camps in the west.
They certainly faired better than the rest.
The North Africa campaign was a major step in the war.
The Axis powers were soon cleared from that tropical shore.
We went into the war with some naive ideas.
We learned along the way how to correct some of these.
Now we had a jumping off place for further war plans.
Sicily seemed a logical next step toward European Lands.

Chapter 4.   Off the Beaten Path

1. Seabees in Action

"Take cover, take cover. I thought we were clear.
The Leathernecks are inland. There should be no Japs near.
Get on the horn. There's a dugout over there.
The bastards waited quietly in their lair.
Where the hell is Raymond? Are the rest of the guys okay?"
"Hey Chief, someone started the dozer. By God it's Ray.
He's got the blade up. He's driving toward the Japs."
The Seabees have a way to take care of a Marine lapse.
Ray moved right up, protecting himself with the blade.
He pushed some dirt and drove up over the barricade.
The Japs inside were buried, no chance to get free.
More dead for the emperor, as it should be.
Within hours of the first Marine hitting the shore,
The Seabees were unloading equipment and more.
By nightfall they'd have part of a runway done.
There'd be an ammo dump, and lights would be strung.
Metal matting was used, less ground to prepare.
Within days fighter aircraft would be landing there.
The Seabees built 111 airstrips in the Pacific alone.
This was just one way that their results shone.
Sometimes it was safe, usually after the Japs were gone.
Otherwise, there was rifle fire, or shells came along.
Occasionally a Jap fighter would make a strafing run.
Then the Seabees took cover 'til he was done.
Nearly 300 lives were lost to enemy fire.
Their efforts to support the troops will always inspire.
They never slacked off though often bone tired.

2. Seabees

The military always depended on a civilian work force

To build all the facilities needed in a war's course.
Since the civilians didn't wear uniforms, they'd be spies.
If they ever were captured, no Geneva rule applies.
The Navy organized <u>C</u>onstruction <u>B</u>attalions early in the war.
They accepted volunteers from 18 to 50 (or more).
Some got in who were over 60 years of age.
They wanted to serve their country (and earn a wage).
Most had experience in one of the building trades
They had worked on highways, bridges, anything that's made.
Early on the Seabees built bases on the northern rout.
Those in Labrador, Greenland, Iceland, England and
   thereabout.
To protect shipping near the Panama Canal Zone,
They built bases where the U-boat attacks were prone.
As we advanced across North Africa and then north,
The Seabees kept up always ready to go forth.
While the European Theater took most of our military might,
A good 80% of the Seabees were in the Pacific fight.
They served on 300 islands or more,
Building airstrips, ammo and fuel dumps, piers on the shore,
Hospitals, warehouses, and barracks for the troops.
As a military team, they were a hell of a group.
When something was in short supply, they made do.
These men were a tremendous inventive crew.
The "moonlight" (or midnight) requisition was perfected,
To save time and red tape. Commanders rarely objected.
Not only did the Seabees always get the job done.
They often did it while under the gun.

3. Inventive Seabees

The Seabees were known for their inventive ways.
One story may be just a tale from the war days.
It seems they were tasked with building an airstrip,
But no steel matting nor even concrete was brought from a
   ship.

41

Someone suggested they use coral from the nearby atoll.
If they kept it wet, maybe they could achieve their goal.
They ground up the coral, some still being alive.
They spread it, and flattened it. It continued to thrive.
Keeping it wet, the coral grew together becoming quite hard.
The airstrip was usable. Ingenuity had its reward.

The pontoon bridge has been in use for two millennia and
    more.
Portable sections are assembled on a river's shore.
The bridge floats. It can take only a limited load.
Still, heavy equipment can utilize this crossing mode.
In the Pacific, floating piers were made of pontoons.
Ships were unloaded faster. It was a real boon.
Someone found another use for loads quite large.
Several sections fastened together became the pontoon barge.

There were always Seabees with that ingenious mind
On Guadalcanal one repaired a discarded find.
He fixed up a machine gun, then found a use.
A Jap Zero strafed their camp, enough abuse.
He fired his gun and brought the plane down.
For a non-combatant he received great renown.
Unfortunately, the Jap navy shelled their base,
And the Seabee hero was in the wrong place.
He received the first Seabee medal of the war.
The posthumous decoration was the Silver Star.

4. Flying Tigers
A year before the war started for the United States
President Roosevelt secretly authorized a fighting group with
    no debate.
Japan was advancing in China. They needed air defense.
Supplying some aircraft and pilots made some sense.
From the Army, Navy, and Marines volunteers came.

Pilots and ground crews stepped forward seeking fame.
These men plus aircraft were sent to Burma nearby
Where they trained with the Curtiss P-40 on the sly.
Two weeks after Pearl Harbor to China they deployed.
First they attacked bombers that they totally destroyed.
They had painted shark faces on each aircraft nose.
They became the Flying Tigers as their fame rose.
There were only 60 aircraft and 100 pilots at most.
At the time their exploits raised the spirits of their host.
The P-40 had two 50 caliber and four 30 caliber guns.
They relied on tactics for all the battles they won.
Their commander, Chennault, insisted that from above they
    should attack.
This helped overcome the P-40's maneuverability lack.
The Jap Zero was better in dog fights it is true,
While we had self sealing gas tanks and pilot armor too.
They relied on spotters to warn them of approaching planes.
The Tigers had time to get enough altitude gains.
They became the 14th Air Force in July of '42.
They lost 14 pilots but downed 300 on the missions they flew.
Americans needed the success provided by this crew.

5. The Hump

Early in the war Japan closed China's access to the sea.
What supplies they got came only from sources three.
First was by road from the USSR in the north,
But this stopped when the USSR-Japan friendship treaty came
    forth.
From the south supplies came up the Burma road.
Then early in '42 the Japs interdicted this mode.
The last supply route was that from the air.
This meant flying from India over the "Hump" to get there.
The Himalayas are the highest mountains on Earth.
Those in the eastern range are lower for what it's worth.
The highest of these are 16,000 feet. This was the "Hump."

None of the pilots cared to hear his plane go "Thump."
"We've got the go ahead. Weather should be clear.
I can see the peaks. We won't fly too near.
This load is lighter than we've had before.
Mostly medical supplies always needed in a war."
They carried fuel for the round trip, a distance of 500 miles.
When they spotted the airfield, it brought out the smiles.
The cargo was unloaded. It didn't take too long,
Then back in the air with the sound of the engine's song.
The only weather information was from other craft.
Many thought to fly this route you had to be daft.
"Captain, we just got a warning, weather from the northwest."
"We haven't enough fuel to return. I'll do my best."
Soon the clouds were thick. They had the feeling of dread.
They'd be flying dead reckoning, with the emphasis on dead.
Then a sudden crash and life's all done.
One second you're alive, the next you're gone.
Some 594 aircraft and 1650 men were lost this way.
Many are still missing to this very day.
Over 42 months they delivered 650,000 tons.
Crossing those desolate mountains on their flying runs.
And helping China fight off the east Asia Huns.

6. Burma

Burma was a British colony before World War II.
They built a highway so supplies could get through.
The Brits were not at war with Japan at the time.
Their material for China partly counteracted Japan's crime.
Over 200,000 Chinese peasants for two long years
Built the Burma Road, through the jungles they cleared
From the port of Rangoon for more than 700 miles,
The road construction certainly presented many trials.
For almost three years trucks traveled the road.
Then Japan overran Rangoon and stopped that supply mode.
General "Vinegar Joe" Stillwell was in that theater of war.

He was helping China reform its army corps.
He and other Americans climbed over mountains tall
To get to India after Burma's fall.
From India's northeast they started another route.
The idea of building the Lido Road caused some doubt.
It had to cross those mountains rather high,
And connect where the north end of the Burma Road lie.
Over 15,000 Americans and 35,000 locals worked on this
    road.
They suffered and died from disease and work overload.
The Lido Road was completed in January of '45.
We know that's late, but the war was still much alive.
We helped an ally fight off Japan's oppression.
China, after all, suffered the most from its aggression.

7. Merrill's Marauders

Our limited presence in Burma ended in '42.
Plans to supply China's army had to be carried through.
General Stillwell ordered Frank Merrill to form a team.
Long range jungle penetration was his scheme.
The Japanese had a fortified town in Burma's north.
This had to be eliminated. The orders were brought forth.
The 5307th Composite Unit was formed then,
Consisting of three battalions with some 1300 men.
In those days there were no helicopters for short hops,
Nor were there clearings suitable for parachute drops.
To approach the enemy meant a long jungle march,
And resupply was difficult. Did the men have the starch?
In Feb of '44 the team started out.
Traveling to attack Myitkyina, the Jap fortified redoubt.
In April, Merrill's Marauders surrounded the town.
A five month siege resulted in their renown.
The 4600 Jap defenders fought to the very last man.
That's how they did it. It was their plan.
With this strategic town secured by our troops,

The Lido Road could be finished by the construction groups.
And Japan could not challenge us with a counter-coup.

8. The Alcan Highway

We needed to replace a bridge in our small town.
It was forecast to take a year. This made me frown.
It crossed a quiet stream less than 20 ft wide.
Why so much time? I started to chide.
They built the Alcan highway in two thirds of a year.
Yes, in war time things happen, it's quite clear.
Then they had to contend with winter's cold.
The following mud season didn't put progress on hold.
From British Columbia, Dawson Creek by name,
It wound over rivers and mountains far from tame.
The total distance was 1400 miles and more.
Well into Alaska, the destination they aimed for.
The bridges were pontoon or made from native wood.
Of course, they cut corners wherever they could.
The surface was corduroy or gravel, of course.
As a military road it could have been worse.
Why did they build it with such speed?
There was the worry Japan would invade Alaska, it was
        agreed.
With the only supply by ship or by air,
We needed a highway to get material there.
When the Japs invaded Attu in June of '42,
It really spurred action with the building crew.
Who did this work at such a rapid pace?
The Army Corps of Engineers were in the race.
They commandeered equipment wherever they could.
They planned as they went, and it worked pretty good.
In later years the road has been vastly improved,
So that adventurous folks can drive it if so moved.
It turned out that Alaska, Japan would not invade,
But the road was built, and records were made.

Why can't our local contractors get as good a grade?

9. Attu Island
In June of '42 the Japanese military had an overall plan.
They were going to invade Midway, but before it began
They wanted to get us to dilute our force.
Their attack on Attu then took its course.
Attu is the most westerly of the Aleutian Chain.
Part of the Alaska Territory, an American claim.
There was no resistance, and we let it go.
The idea is we'd accept this minor blow,
And concentrate our force for the Midway fight,
Which we figured was almost in sight.
The Japs had a secondary invasion excuse.
Attu could be a base for later offensive use,
And in case the Russians joined us in the war,
They could intercept commerce between our shores.
We decided to take back Attu in May of '43.
We could use it for our own base, you see.
This island was not ideal to attack with beaches bad,
And the permafrost was not good for the vehicles we had.
Though it's usual for the attackers to lose more,
The Japs casualties were 50% greater in the island war.
Partly this was due to a massive banzai charge.
Of all the Pacific action, this was the most large.
Because of the fight on that day,
The battle site has the new name "Massacre Bay."
The airfield on Attu, we went on to expand,
And then aircraft attacked the Kuril Islands north of Japan.
The Attu campaign was a sidelight of the total affair,
Except for the 1600 who lost their lives there.

10. Coast Watchers
"Ferdinand the Bull," is the title of a children's story.
He liked to smell the flowers with no thought of any glory.

47

It was also the code name of the coast watchers group.
They watched, took note and reported any scoop.
Their duty was to be unobtrusive, to stay out of sight.
Like Ferdinand, if they were stung, then they could fight.
There were over 300 islands in the Solomon chain.
Coast watchers hid out and reported ships and planes.
They radioed the information to the best of their knowledge
To Naval and Marine bases to give them an edge.
"Betties (24) and Zeroes (16) flying out from Rabaul.
They just passed my position, signing off, Paul."
Of course, so the Japs wouldn't know, this was in code.
The receivers knew from the message what it forebode.
Our fighters would be airborne with a preemptive attack.
With luck we'd down the bombers or force them to turn back.
This meant we would limit damage to ship and base.
We won battles there. Guadalcanal was the place.
Admiral Halsey gave credit where credit was due.
We might not have won there without the coast watching crew.
Who were these men who risked their lives this way?
If they were caught, with their lives they would pay.
Australian military, escaped POWs, civilians and more.
Even three German missionaries wanted to help even the
  score.
The play, "South Pacific" helped propagate their lore.

11. Code Talkers
"Alpha company needs "potatoes" and "finger sticks*"
Sixteen "table cases*" ready, need "pregnant air."
This means hand grenades and 50 caliber rounds,
Sixteen wounded for evac and need bombers hitting the
  ground.
Think of this message in alphabet cipher code,
And spoken in the Navajo language, a complex mode.
Actually, a native born Navajo couldn't decode this
Unless he had memorized the code book lists.

Code talking started informally in World War I.

The Cherokee and Choctaw troops helped defeat the Hun.

Hitler (Crazy White Man) heard of this and sent 30 to learn.

Too hard a job, but in Europe their use was spurned,

Except for Meskwaki code talkers. They enlisted together in
      '41.

They were used in North Africa 'til that campaign was done.

Also, Comanche landed in Normandy with the Fourth
      Division troops.

Their time was limited by too many wounded in the group.

The biggest contingent were Navajo Marines in the Pacific.

Their mission was planned early. The results were terrific.

Only about 30 non-Navajo, this language could understand.

It was unwritten, and it was only used on tribal lands.

About 200 were recruited in May of '42.

The first group created the Navajo Code, it's true.

They picked unique descriptive names, not a prank.

Like sewing machine for machine gun and turtle for tank.

Periodically, reps from each division would have a meet

To select new words and to keep the code uniform and neat.

In the Iwo Jima campaign six code talkers worked round the
      clock.

They sent 800 messages in two days. Later when taking stock,

A signal officer stated, "Without them we wouldn't have won
      here."

Maybe overstated, but he wanted to make it clear.

Only one Navajo was taken a prisoner of war.

The code talkers were organized in May, this was before.

The Japs tortured him to find how to read the code.

They never broke him. The warrior in him showed.

A recent movie said no code talker would ever be taken alive,

And there was a fellow Marine to make sure he didn't survive.

If you think about this, you'll agree it's a lot of jive.

*Made up names.

Chapter 5.   We're Behind You

1. The Pentagon
The war was coming and everyone knew.
Forward thinkers were aware of all they needed to do.
The War and Navy departments were in temporary buildings
    on the Mall.*
Constructed for World War I, they were much too small.
With military expansion we would need office space.
One of two plots across the Potomac would be the place.
The first selected plot had an area with five sides.
Thus, the pentagon shape building was what was tried.
With steel being in short supply due to the war,
Reinforced concrete was specified. It was limited to five floors.
President Roosevelt vetoed the first chosen site.
They kept the pentagon shape as you'd expect they might.
Ground was broken on Sept. 11 of '41.**
Like other war projects, construction was quickly done.
In 16 months the world's largest*** office building was
    complete.
Often the construction preceded the design in this feat.
The Pentagon has five stories above and two below ground.
There are five ring corridors that circle around.
The floor area is 6.5 million square feet.
This is equal to 4000 homes on a typical street.
26,000 workers, military and civilian, work there.
With 17.5 miles of corridors, they have to take care.
If they should get lost, it would cause quite a scare.
The Pentagon is still busy as we are well aware.
* These were still there in the fifties.
** Precisely 60 years prior to 9/11.
***At the time it was the largest building in the world and still
    is the largest office building. The 747 assembly building

in Washington State and the NASA assembly building in
Florida now exceed its volume.

2. Dollar-a-Year Men
Managers were in great need early in the war.
Many leaders of business wanted to do more.
They flocked to Washington to do their share.
The President needed them. Their talents were rare.
The Federal Government had to plan so many ways.
We needed war production started in the early days.
To avoid inflation, we needed to control each price.
With demand for workers, we had to entice.
Materials had to be reallocated from peacetime needs.
With the mobilization this required speed.
The heads of GE, Ford, GM, and Sears to name a few,
Helped to get the country moving, quite a crew.
It was a real sacrifice, their pay, one dollar per year.
No bouses, no stock options, their patriotism was clear.
Could this happen now if the country were in need?
The doubt is pretty strong, too much unbridled greed.

3. The North Platte Canteen
In the old days North Platte, Nebraska had its renown,
Violence, gambling, houses of ill repute, a pretty rough town.
Something happened very early in World War II.
People knew that a troop train was passing through.
This was Company D of the Nebraska National Guard.
These boys would be facing a life pretty hard.
Over 500 people gathered with letters, candy, and food.
But they were Kansas soldiers. It didn't change the mood.
Rae, a 26 year old, hoped to see her brother that day.
She had the "Great Idea", a eureka moment you could say.
They formed a committee, and on Christmas eight days later,
A handful greeted a troop train at 11:00 PM . What could be
      greater?

Within two weeks they had a lunch room and had met 9000
    troops.
There was food and words of encouragement for each group.
Soon the canteen was open from 5:00AM 'til the last train.
An average of 4000 per day* stopped at the town in the plains.
55,000 volunteers from 125 towns out there
Kept it going for all the years of the war.
For the GIs train travel was a form of hell.
Five days sitting up to cross the country if it went well,
No showers, no breaks, only military rations to eat,
Then came a few moments of heaven from those that they'd
    meet,
Tables piled high with home made food and drink,
Bibles, books, and magazines were provided more than you'd
    ever think,
Words of encouragement when they were fearful of what's to
    come,
Treated like heroes when they felt pretty glum.
All this was provided, and they never charged a dime.
People gave of their hearts, their wallets, and their time.
Thinking of all war's cruelty, is there hope for the human
    race?
Yes, when you think of the kindness of this small place.
For them we can have a tear in each eye and a smile on every
    face.
*Six million total.

4. The USO
The USO to those who are about my age,
Is the picture of Bob Hope on an open air stage.
Stretched before him is an ocean of young GIs,
Intent on his jokes and cracks that are wise.
Bob Hope and his troupe were one of a host
Who put on shows at hospitals, bases, and posts.
But that's not all the USO did. Besides the groups,

They provided a little bit of home for the troops.
There was coffee and donuts, movies, dances and more,
A place where the guys could go and forget the war.
The United Service Organizations was started in early '41.
Roosevelt requested it of six groups* and so it was begun.
Tom Dewey, the Presidential candidate in '48,
Was the first chairman. He was followed by other greats.
It's estimated that 300,000 performances were made
In just about every war zone in sun and shade.
Sometimes there was rain and wind, but no one fled.
"The show must go on," as it's always been said.
Twenty eight performers died while on the tour.
Glenn Miller, the band leader, we'll remember for sure.
The USO is still here. Their mission will endure.
* The Salvation Army, YMCA, YWCA, The National Jewish
   Welfare Board, The National Catholic Community
   Service, and The National Travelers Aid Assoc.

5. The Red Cross
"Hey, Sarge, there's a truck coming through the gate.
Maybe they have some food. That would be great.
No, it's that guy from the Red Cross we've seen before.
He's got the mail pouch. I could sure use some more."
"I've got a letter from home. I'll read it to you.
'All OK. Joey appendix out. Bill Marines, Oct. two.
Molly six puppies three girls. Marge all A's fifth.
Got letter. Have faith. All send love.' That's a real gift."
All messages or letters were limited to 25 words.
The rule was family news only which seems absurd.
The Red Cross delivered 24 million to prisoners of war.
These were mostly in Europe. The Japs had a closed door.
Some parcels got through with medicines and food.
This only was allowed if a country was in the mood.
The Germans, though bastards, let the Red Cross through.
Japan and Russia did as you'd expect they'd do.

The Japs sank a Red Cross ship, a senseless slaughter.
They said no foreign vessels allowed in their waters.
The Red Cross visited German POW camps to inspect.
They reported bad treatment, though this had no effect.
Over the years the Red Cross pushed for civilian rights,
Those arrested or deported, slave laborers, the result of war's
    fights.
They had no luck with a treaty as you'd expect they might.

6. The OSS

"Gentlemen don't read each other's mail," the quote
From Secretary of State Stimson, the silly old goat.
This was in peace time back in '29.
With no war on the horizon this seemed fine.
We did have rudimentary information gathering before the
    war.
The FBI, the Navy, the War Department and more,
They each found out info, but didn't share.
Fortunately, there was code breaking as you're aware.
Roosevelt asked "Wild" Bill Donovan to study the need
For a global intelligence gathering network with the highest
    speed.
The Office of Strategic Services or OSS was formed in June
    '42.
Wild Bill was coordinator of information. Everything was
    new.
Their primary job was to make estimates and learn facts.
No James Bond super spy was part of the act.
One activity that was outside their normal purview
Was the arming and training of Mao's Chinese and Viet Minh
    too.
The theory that my enemy's enemy is my friend
Worked against the Japs until the war's end.
We had up to 24,000 in the OSS at is peak.
Gathering and evaluating information, all they would seek.

Throughout occupied Europe there were watching spies.
They transmitted facts like, "Division 28 is moving by."
Sometimes a bigger picture resulted from each related bit.
The analyst's job was to make it all fit.
The penetrating operatives in Nazi Germany hid out.
Don't bring attention to yourself. Be a scout.
How much they helped the war effort no one can say.
But they risked their lives in every way.
Some famous OSS workers of which you may have heard,
Arthur Schlesinger, Julia Child, Allen Dulles*, Arthur
    Goldberg.
One of their training facilities was Camp David, the
    Presidential retreat.
The OSS was disbanded just after Japan's defeat.
However, after discovering the Soviet spy network in the USA,
They reconstituted the OSS to become the CIA.
*Brother of Secretary of State, John Foster Dulles.

7. WASPS (Women Air Force Service Pilots)

The Army Air Corps didn't want them for sure.
Even though the shortage of male pilots they'd help cure.
Some 25 women traveled to Britain to do their bit.
In the Air Transport Auxiliary, they certainly fit.
Finally, two organizations* were combined in '43.
Some 25,000 volunteered. To help fight was their plea.
About 1800 were selected for the pilot training school,
And 60% of these made it, though their treatment was cruel.
The women paid for their own transportation there.
There was no lodging and damn little care.
No uniforms were provided. The training planes were a mix.
They persevered and finished no matter the Air Corps' tricks.
The WASPS were in existence for a year and a third,
When the top brass gave them the final word.
They'd ferried almost 13,000 planes from factory to base,
Even crossing the Atlantic to more than one place.

They towed targets for antiaircraft gun fire,
Certainly a dangerous task. They should be admired.
Women pilots even flew the new B-29,
Proving to male pilots that it handled fine.
They practiced strafing runs, cargo transport, all with no
	gripes,
Sixty million miles flown on 78 aircraft types.
38 died by accident and were sent home at family expense.
No honors, no coffin flag, we should all be incensed.
They were a civilian outfit, the military said.
At least they could have recognized the dead.
The records were sealed 'til '77 when at last
Women pilots were accepted, and they took note of the past.
Finally, military status was given to these brave souls.
The WASPS were outstanding. They had filled their roles.
Note: early on they called themselves "the Guinea Pigs."
Then "Fifinella," the female gremlin. They weren't prigs.
They should have been more accepted by the military
	bigwigs.
*WAFS (Women's Auxiliary Ferrying Squadron) and WFTD
	(Women's Flying Training Detachment)

8. Rosie the Riveter

We love you, Rosie. It's sexy to be tough.
As they say about men, you have the right stuff.
In the '40s many of the skilled men went to war.
Women and other untrained got onto the factory floor.
Some had the soft jobs as theirs, of course,
But they also took those requiring physical force.
They welded, they assembled, they used the riveting gun.
They worked overtime 'til the job was done.
Early on, the government realized they needed women
	workers.
They also wanted the young, the old, farmers. There were no
	shirkers.

They used two lady models showing their charm.
Most are familiar with Rosie and her muscular arm.
Her motto was, "We can do it." Of power she had the most.
The second riveter appeared on the cover of the Saturday
	Evening Post.
I really don't know how our workers performed so well.
They produced huge quantities for the Axis' death knell.
On these pages you'll read about manufactures in surfeit.
We armed 12 million of ours, plus aiding the Russians and the
	Brits.
It has been said the women's movement got its start
With the wartime work. They did such an important part.
Of course, the ladies lost their jobs with the war's end.
Returning GIs needed work. There was no defense money to
	spend.
A postscript from our modern age and day.
Rosie posters can be found in places out of the way.
Young Moslem women want equality without delay.

9. Missing

"Mom, I miss Dad a lot. Where did he go?"
"Your Dad's in the war. That you already know.
We got that telegram. They said he's MIA.
That means missing in action. It's what they say.
We can only hope he's in a hospital somewhere.
He lost his memory and dog tags before going there.
We can pray he remembers when he comes to,
And he tells the doctor. They'll know what to do.
Maybe he's on a deserted island way out at sea,
Or a prisoner of war, and someday he'll be free.
Now get ready for bed and say your prayers."
"Mom, I forgot last night. Do you think God cares?
Maybe God won't help to find my Dad,
Because I forgot. I've been really bad."
"You're the best son anyone ever had.

God will help if he can. You're my sweet lad."

10. Dear John

Thanks for all the letters. I hope that you get mine.
Are you still on the base? Staying there is fine.
It may be tiresome, and it doesn't seem like war,
Thank your lucky stars, it's better that you're bored.
Mom's out of the hospital. She seemed a little weak.
It was touch and go for a while. Her chances seemed bleak.
She's getting stronger each day, even cooked a bit.
Dad was upset. When he found out, he had a fit.
He's been working six, ten hour days a week.
With overtime his wages have hit a peak.
Jimmy is going steady with Rosie from school.
You may remember her brother Eddie. He's kinda cool.
He's talking about enlisting like you. He has no doubts.
Everyone wants him to wait. He's afraid he'll miss out.
Otherwise, the family is all fine. We're getting by.
When I hear about some folks, I want to cry.
I have some news that you won't like to hear.
I met a guy, and he can be sweet and dear.
He's a cop in town. He doesn't have to worry about the draft.
He's always here for me. You may think I'm daft.
It's Ralph Sweeney. We have made big plans.
So I'm breaking up with you. Can you understand?
Ralph doesn't like my writing, so this is the last one.
Good luck and stay safe until the war's all done.
I know you are hurt, but that's not what I intend.
Maybe in the future, we can be each other's friend.
Even so, I'll seal this with a kiss.

                           Your new friend. Just call me Sis.
                           Sally

11. Willie and Joe

They were two "Dogfaces," infantry men, GIs,

Created by Bill Mauldin who was one of the guys.
Before the war, Bill had formal training in the arts.
Joining the National Guard was how he got his military start.
For the 45th Division newspaper, Mauldin was a volunteer.
He drew cartoons which gave the troops cheer.
The Stars and Stripes, the soldiers newspaper, brought him
  on board.
Mauldin's cartoons coming out six times a week were the GIs'
  reward.
Willie and Joe had a week of whiskery growth.
They were grimy and unkempt and could utter an oath
The Dogfaces loved them. Not so the top brass.
Patton even threatened Mauldin, "I'll jail his ass.*"
Old time officers were of the spit and shine school.
Soldiers must be clean shaven. That's the rule.
Patton was after him for spreading dissent,
Until Eisenhower said to cool it. It's not his intent.
His cartoons gave the soldiers an outlet from their hell.
When the paper arrived, humor helped break the spell.
Bill Mauldin told an interviewer, and I'll tell you.
I'll quote it directly since no rhyme will do.
"I always admired Patton. Oh, sure the stupid bastard was
  crazy.
He was insane. He thought he was living in the dark ages.
Soldiers were peasants to him. I didn't like that attitude..."
Mauldin got a Pulitzer Prize for his book "Up Front,"
Cartoons and impassioned telling how life was for the grunts.
*Not a direct quote.

12. Kilroy

Wherever the GIs went, there was a message clear.
Some unknown guy wrote, "Kilroy was here."
Accompanying it was a drawing of a guy most bald,
Only his top part was visible as he peaked over a wall.
The Australians had their favorite named "Foo."

The Brits' "Mr. Chad" appeared frequently too.
The Germans saw the message and thought it was code.
Was there a secret mission coming down the road?
How did it start? Many have tried to find out.
There's a good explanation though there's always doubt.
Mr. J. J. Kilroy was an inspector in Quincy, Mass.
In the Fore River Shipyard, the welding had to pass.
After inspecting the work for each section of ship,
He'd write his name in chalk so he wouldn't skip.
Also, this is so the welders wouldn't cheat,
And claim more work, the pay system to beat.
So each ship that went off to war
Had "Kilroy" written by the score.
Did J. J. realize the sensation he created?
I doubt he knew how his name was fated.

13. SNAFU
The word SNAFU was invented early in the war,
As a young GI's reaction to acronyms galore.
The military had enough but always thought up more.
It means that the normal situation is a bad state.
We don't mince words, we give it to you straight.
Our lives couldn't be worse. This is our fate.
We can say politely, "Situation normal, all fouled up."
But the Navy like, "Situation normal, the Army f...... up."
While the Army retorted, "Some Navy a.... f.... up."
Also, there's, "F.... up beyond all recognition, " or FUBAR.
Does SUSFU, "Situation unchanged, still f.... up," go too far?
These were the popular ones. There certainly were more.
Now it seems SNAFU describes almost any mistake.
We all hope it's not the norm for goodness sake.
Maybe WASU for, "What a screw up," is enough for now,
Since SNAFU is too extreme for most mistakes somehow.

Chapter 6.   Southwest Pacific, 1943

1. Surprise

"We got the okay. They went right to the top.
Tomorrow's the day. Just hope we don't have to stop."
A message had been decoded. It was a really big deal.
Admiral Yamamoto was traveling. We could get him for real,
We had the departure, the destination, and the time of each.
We could get the bum. He would be in our reach.
President Roosevelt, no less, had approved the mission.
Yamamoto was big enough that we needed permission.
No one wanted the Japs to know how much we could read.
We would have to make it appear this was an unplanned deed.
Sixteen P-38 fighters were assigned to the assassination try.
Four were the "Killer Section," with 12 for cover up high.
The P-38 Lightning was the only plane with enough range
To fly the round trip from Henderson Field for the aerial
      exchange.
They took off early and stayed close to the deck,
Less observable to the Japs against the sea, just specks.
Radio silence was broken at the Bougainville coast.
"Bogies, 11 o'clock high," the Japs would be toast.
There were two light bombers (Betties) instead of one,
And a flock of Zeroes to participate in the fun.
After aerial acrobatics both bombers went down,
And five of the six Zeroes crashed, water or earth bound.
One of the "Killers" didn't make it back.
Another had over 100 bullet holes from Zero attacks.
Why Yamamoto? For the Jap military he was top man.
He planned the Pearl Harbor attack when the war began.
Was this payback or to impress the leadership of Japan?

2. Pilot Down

"He's on my tail. Crap I'm taking hits.
Rpms are dropping. She's coughing a bit.
Stopped, dead. I'll try to get it started again.
I'm at 5,000 feet. I have a few seconds, maybe ten.
That's it. I'm out of here. Get the canopy loose.
Seat belt off. Hope I miss the tail. Now it's vamoose.
They say we should drop as far as we dare.
Less time for the Japs to take target practice up there.
Okay. I'm pulling the cord. Not dropping too far is best.
Wet landing. Get the chute straps off. Inflate the Mae West.*
Where the hell am I? That island may belong to the Japs.
Hope I don't float too close. They're rather nasty chaps.
By God my buddies are still flying around.
They'll keep the Jap bastards from a pilot who's downed.
Some of the guys have been strafed at sea.
They'll do their damnedest to keep it from happening to me.
What's that splash? I hear a gun report.
Don't tell me a shore battery is using me for sport.
By God, my guys are going after that gun.
Don't mess with Marine Air. It won't be fun.
They've got to be running low on fuel. They'll leave.
Then my goose will be cooked, I do believe.
What! I see more planes coming over that cloud.
I'm not alone. It's time for a prayer. I'm allowed."
His buddies dropped him a life raft and then a chute.
This would be a sea anchor to keep him from the brutes.
A PBY arrived, It taxied to his side.
He climbed aboard thankful for the ride.
The Japs opened up and shot off the tail.
It was the last thing they did before they were nailed.
Marine Air protected the pilot and now the PBY crew.
Finally, a speedy PT boat cruised into view.
All airmen rescued was the goal shown here.
Let the Japs ponder. We hold our men's lives dear.

*A life jacket that makes the wearer look busty.

3. The Hero of Arundel

The destroyer Strong was sinking fast.
She was hit by a torpedo. It could have gone past.
It was launched by a Jap ship 13 miles away.
Our ship was not the target on that fateful day.
The men were evacuating to another ship nearby.
Lieutenant Hugh was helping trapped sailors not to die.
An explosion knocked him out. He came to at sea.
Amongst a cluster of men, broken rafts and other debris.
Hugh was the ranking officer. He took charge of the band.
He ordered some men to paddle away in search of land.
They were at the mercy of the currents flowing there.
Men were dying, their wounds they could no longer bear.
Five had survived when they landed on a beach.
Water and food were found and within reach.
This was the island of Arundel in the Solomon group.
Hugh realized that it was occupied by Japanese troops.
He ordered the three remaining men to seek aid.
The fourth had died. Hugh felt his own life fade.
While reconnoitering, he found a dead Jap, a relief.
His shoes fit, there were two grenades, and some tinned beef.
Though suffering from internal injuries and in pain,
Hugh started after the Japs, his personal campaign.
One grenade he used to kill a five man patrol.
They had rifles, ammo and grenades. He was on a role.
Later he wiped out several machine gun nests.
The incensed Japs sent patrols to eliminate the pest.
They never found him even though he left a sign.
A passing US plane spotted it. Was their guidance Devine?
An amphibius plane landed. They sent a raft ashore.
After 43 days alone, Hugh was rescued. Could you ask for
    more?
One thought you should keep in mind about him as he hid.

63

Hugh was a Naval officer never trained in what he did.

4. The Battle of the Bismark Sea*
The Japs had evacuated Guadalcanal to the east.
On New Guinea they needed to reinforce at least.
They'd still be in position to attack Australia at a later date.
As long as they held on, they'd be blessed by fate.
They planned a convoy from Rabaul for resupply.
This would include eight troop transports guarded by
Eight destroyers and 100 planes from nearby fields.
However, we decrypted messages, so their fate was sealed.
As they wended their way southward bound,
Our search aircraft hunted 'til they were found.
We started our attack with B-17s from 5000 feet.
They did sink one transport of the 16 ship fleet.
Unfortunately, a Zero fighter shot down a Flying Fort.
He machine gunned the survivors, a type of sport.
Later B-17s gave another try but didn't do much.
High altitude bombs went wide. The ships weren't touched.
We sent in torpedo bombers and B-25s, everything we had.
Finally, the battle was done, but some results were sad.
We machine gunned Japs at sea. It was pay back time.
They had done it to us, but it was clearly a crime.
All transports were sunk, of the destroyers, four.
The Japs also lost 20 aircraft to complete the score.
Our losses were 13 men and six aircraft down,
A one sided victory which earned us our renown.
But MacArthur wouldn't leave the reporting at that.
His office doubled the numbers by commander's fiat.
*Mar. 2-4, 1943

5. New Guinea
Where is this place? Can you find it on the map?
Only a few know of or remember our fight there with the Japs.
It's the second biggest island in the world, length 1600 miles.

Fighting began there in '42 with tribulations and trials.
The Australians fought alone. We fought the Japs on
    Guadalcanal.
It took six months before we joined our Aussie pals.
What a hell of a place to fight two simultaneous wars,
Both the Japs and the jungle and what it had in store.
"It rains daily for nine months and then the monsoon starts,"
Recalled a vet. If you fought there, you were not too smart.
There was malaria and other tropical diseases of every sort.
If you wanted to complain, there was no need to distort.
There were no roads or rails outside of towns,
Only jungle paths from the seacoast to the mountain crowns.
Traveling overland was impossible for any sizeable force.
You had to carry all you needed. What could be worse?
We walked in knee deep mud, hefted a sixty pound pack,
And expected and got a hidden enemy attack.
To get around this, we imagined New Guinea was like a sea.
The coastal settlements were islands, the only place jungle
    free.
So we hopped from one spot to the next and built an airfield
    there.
This was so we would always have control of the air.
Our procedure worked, especially when we surprised the
    Japs,
And blasted parked aircraft when defenders had a lapse.
It was a shoestring operation with limited landing craft.
We proceeded along the north coast even using rafts.
Two years were spent conquering this land.
We even bypassed areas occupied by Jap bands.
Just think of the poor guys serving in this command.
Another invasion and then again. How much can you stand?

6. Hollandia

With determination our military moved up the New Guinea
    coast.

On occasion things worked so well, you'd like to boast.
Air raids were planned against Jap airfields.
Three in the Hollandia area promised a good yield.
A flight of B-24 bombers escorted with P-38s
Caught the Japs unaware. Disaster was their fate.
Sometimes the big bombers just flat out miss.
That's why they're not so good against bridges and ships.
Airfields are big and with luck and skill
You can hit parked aircraft and get many a kill.
Our bombers each made their pass. The P-38s had a go.
Their strafing runs were the final blow.
Weeks later our invading infantry counted the score.
They found plane graveyards with 340 junked or more.
In one attack, we guaranteed superiority in the air.
For the southwest Pacific, Japan had no planes to spare.

7. Jungle Trek

"All Churchill has to offer is blood sweat and tears.
Blood and tears I can take. Sweat, there's too much here.
It rains all the time, so the humidity is high.
Add heated temperature, and you can understand why
I sweat so much my clothes are always wet.
Of all my experiences, this I'd like most to forget.
Since my uniform and skin just never dry out,
Jungle rot, athletes' foot, jock itch, are a continuous bout.
While I'm on the subject, let me moan and bitch.
What's worse, blood sucking leaches or mosquitos? I don't
	know which.
Is it malaria or anemia that makes me so weak?
With nothing but C-rations, life is so bleak.
The mud never stops except when wading through streams.
Get me out of here, Lord. I'm going to scream.
I promise myself before God and man, I swear
If I ever get home, I'll live in a cold desert somewhere.
And yet, when I look at this great profusion of life

For a brief time I forget the war and its strife.
The birds are so beautiful with colors bright.
I'm amazed by the orchids. What a memorable sight.
Take away the predatory varmints that make life hell,
Maybe less rain and mud, maybe a better smell,
And it wouldn't be too bad. I could tarry a spell.

8. The Northern Solomons

Our plan was to expand control of the Solomon Isles.
Gaining land for building airfields was our style.
New Georgia was the first, invaded in June of '43.
The Marines had less resistance than they thought there'd be.
The airfield was quickly constructed to help in the fight.
Then the main force landed to seal the Japs' plight.
It took two months to complete the campaign.
Then they got ready to do it all over again.
Resistance often was tough. Jungle fighting is like that,
Two months rest, then on to the next combat.
This was a combined effort with Aussies and Kiwis.*
There even was a contingent from the Island of Fiji.
Bougainville was next, New Britain followed then.
The Marines went in first, being the landing trained men.
Soon Army and Australian units took their place.
Then a policy shift changed the war's pace.
Both islands were neutralized, no need to win.
In a year and a half the Japs surrendered, all done in.
Rabaul, the mighty Jap base, no longer was the goal.
It was isolated with no resupply. It no longer had a role.
The islands' surrender was just prior to Japan's.
Most likely the atom bombs decided their plans.
*New Zealanders

9. Cemetery Duty

Back from the next invaded island, he climbed the hill.
Though the offshore breeze was up, all seemed still.

The crosses and stars were lined up just so.
The Seabees do neat work when not on the go.
A slim man ambled up. He opened the gate.
"Can I help you sir, maybe someone I can locate.?"
"Just looking around. Who's that with all the flowers?"
"That's our commander, like a father, that was his power.
He was a good man. Everyone here was good, everyone.
What are we going to do when the good are all done?"
"Maybe enough good ones will survive this war.
Maybe when we need them, there'll be more.
I hear they may move them all back to the States."
"I hope they don't. That wouldn't be so great.
This is the perfect place with the sea so vast.
The stars fill the night sky. It's more than you could ask.
In the heat of day it's cooled by the breeze.
Off on the side, there's shade from the jungle trees.
Here they're surrounded by heroes and friends.
They're all good men who have met their end.
There's guys here from each ethnic group and race.
Nowhere else can you find a spot to take its place.
The Lord has blessed them with his grace."
Who is that man? I'll ask as soon as I can.
Why, back in Georgia he's called the preacher man.

Chapter 7.   Europe, 1943

1. The Man Who Never Was
We all should be glad the Brits were on our side.
They were really devious. Of this they should take pride.
The MI5 agency* pulled more than one trick on the Hun.
But that's for another book after this one's done.
We had plans to invade Sicily after the African campaign.
This was so obvious our intent would be plain.
However, well in advance a ruse was planned
That might convince the Germans of another place we'd land.
Both Sardinia and Greece would do for this plot.
Information to this end was leaked as the designated spot.
First MI5 found the body of a derelict bum.
He had no known relatives, and his death was kept mum.
One William Martin, Major, Royal Marines was born.
He was a courier. All was proper in how he was adorned.
He carried letters to generals and other important papers,
Plus personal stuff that made it a realistic caper.
His body was dropped by a sub near the coast of Spain,
Though everyone would believe he came from the wreck of a
    plane.
Spain was Germany's friend though neutral in the war.
It was hoped the Germans would examine the corpse and
    what he bore.
The Spanish provided it, and the Germans copied it all.
But they did so carefully, no detail too small.
To the British Attache, they delivered the body and his case.
Then the Brits examined it again, every last trace.
They determined that all items had been opened and read.
The ruse had worked with all the information fed.
The Germans did remove troops from Sicily as planned.
The invasion went ahead, and the results were grand.

After the invasion the Germans knew they were fooled.
Later they got true information and false it was ruled.
In years, "The man who never was" got a name.
Glyndwr Michael, as Major Martin, then got his fame.
*MI5 employed Ian Fleming, creator of James Bond.

2. The Invasion of Sicily
The British had their ruse to fake out the Hun.
For it to work they had to keep at it 'til Sicily was won.
So we bombed airfields all over Sardinia and Greece,
Plus Sicily and the Italian mainland. It didn't cease.
Just after midnight on the tenth of July, the mission began.
Two British and two American forces started the plan.
Unfortunately, our aircraft flew over the offshore fleet.
Nervous Naval gunners thought it was an attack and in their
        heat,
They shot down 23 of our transport planes.
Over 300 Airborne died. This error was insane.
The Brits with their gliders had a similar catastrophe.
Only 12 reached the target while 69 crashed at sea.
Due to high winds, the paratroopers were scattered.
They used their initiative in places where it mattered.
They held bridges, attacked patrols, and created panic and
        confusion.
Things didn't go as planned, but worked is the conclusion.
Amphibious landings were spread over 105 miles of beach.
These were on the south and east. Did we overreach?
Even with high winds and sand bars, we got our men ashore.
Maybe in the wrong place, maybe late, mistakes happen in
        war.
The invasion set two records never matched in any fray,
The longest landing zone and seven divisions landed in one
        day.
We learned a few things for later invasion plans.
Make sure the landing zone has no bars of sand,

And don't have paratroopers fly over the fleet toward land.

3. Sicily's Liberation

No landing was expected since the weather was foul.
There was fog and rain, and the wind howled.
The Italian commander didn't want to fight on the beech.
He had no desire to be within the Naval guns' reach.
The Americans landed three divisions under General Patton's
    command.
Their goal was to drive north and divide this land.
One Canadian and three British divisions with General
    Montgomery's lead
Were tasked to block the Nazi escape with speed.
It was necessary that the Brits take Medina, the port,
While Patton would then drive eastward. Would the plan
    come up short?
The Nazis shortened their defense line in the northeast.
They slowed the Brit's advance. It just about ceased.
Patton's army advanced with several amphibious landings.
He drove his men. Some even slept while standing.
Then Montgomery knowing the Nazis were getting away,
Removed men from the line to train for the next foray.
The trap never closed. Almost half the defenders went to sea,
And landed on the Italian coast. They had gotten free.
The evacuation was well planned with concentrated guns,
Both antiaircraft and antiship to safeguard their boat runs.
The Medina straight is just three miles wide.
All those evacuated were available to fight on the other side.
Patton was incensed at Montgomery's failure to proceed.
This would not be the last time he would not succeed.
We liberated Sicily which controlled the central
    Mediterranean Sea.
It took 38 days, the New Hampshire sized island to free.
We found the Italian soldiers had no loyalty to their regime.
This was the German's war, or so it would seem.

In fact their Mussolini was soon toppled from power.
His dictatorial rule had long ago soured.
Some have suggested that the Mafia helped us out.
There's no evidence of this though they had some clout.

4. George S. Patton

Born into a family that was military to the core.
Ancestors fought for the South in the Civil War.
Patton aimed his whole life to continue this line.
He graduated from West Point in the class of '09.
The military still used horse cavalry on that date.
As a horseman, marksman, and fencer, Patton was great.
He competed in the pentathlon at the Olympic Games.
He came in fifth because of scoring, a shame.
At pistol firing he really had a perfect score,
But the judges said no, of holes they needed more.
They wouldn't believe a shot went through an existing hole.
Patton accepted this as a gentleman, though his medal they
        stole.
He developed techniques and a new saber for the cavalry.
That's how the nickname "Old Blood and Guts" came to be.
Patton rode with Pershing on the Poncho Villa campaign.
Then fought in World War I. Cavalry had no use, it was plain.
He learned about tanks and commanded the same.
This became his driving passion in the war game.
When World War II started, Patton was on the fast track.
He commanded the Western Force in the North Africa attack.
After our disastrous loss in the Battle of Kasserine Pass,
Patton took over. Soon we gave the Nazis a blast.
He successfully lead our forces in the Sicily invasion.
We drove back the Axis on every occasion.
Patton toured a hospital to check on the wounded GIs.
He wanted to thank them but got a surprise.
One soldier had no wounds that could be seen,
So Patton slapped and berated him. He was rather mean.

One nurse was incensed and had to be held back.
She meant to stop the General in his attack.
The media learned of this and spread the news.
Patton lost his command because of his short fuze.
Would we lose our best general due to this stupid act,
Even though he apologized? He didn't know the facts.
The soldier had battle fatigue and a case of malaria too.
He wasn't a slacker. He forgave Patton. Wouldn't you?
However, Patton was on the sidelines for almost a year.
Strangely, this helped us in ways I'll later make clear.

5. Old Blood and Guts

After the "incident" Ike thought of sending him back to the
    States.
Instead, cooling his heels was Patton's fate.
For the warrior this was worse than death.
He'd wanted combat from his very first breath.
The unintended result was confusion in the German
    command.
Why was our very best general being canned?
Ike kept him in Sicily. The Hun thought he'd invade the south
    of France.
Patton stayed in Cairo, a Balkan invasion was a good chance.
Months before D-Day Ike made him commander of the First
    Army Group.
This fictional army helped the Germans be duped.
They expected Calais would be our main invasion route.
Normandy was but a feint. Hitler especially had no doubt.
After D-Day the Third Army became Patton's command.
Along the beachhead, this was on the far right hand.
He was back in his glory, no ifs, and, or buts.
A quote from the troops, "Our blood and his guts."
They loved the old bastard. They must have been nuts.

6. Salerno Italy*

Soon after the conquest of Sicily was done,
We invaded Italy, the next operation against the Hun.
Crossing the Medina straight, the Brits started the attack.
Landing craft could go directly forth and then come back.
No need for larger ships to load the small boats.
The three mile wide straight required little time afloat.
The Germans fell back as Montgomery had thought.
They blocked roads and cut bridges. Few battles were fought.
Six days later GIs and Brits landed on Salerno beaches.
It's 300 miles north. Fighters from Sicily were within reach.
Naples was nearby which would provide a good port.
We needed this so supplies wouldn't be short.
Before the invasion we didn't blast away.
The Army wanted to surprise the defenders of Naples Bay.
But the Hun wasn't surprised as we soon discovered.
"Come on in and give up. We have you covered."
A loudspeaker blared as we approached the landing.
We didn't give up though the voice was demanding.
Some units had an easy time going ashore.
They moved inland to block mountain passes and more.
Other units had a harder time but got Naval aid.
Ship guns blasted away in a regular cannonade.
We had support from aircraft with control of the air.
The Nazi defenders were soon pushed out of there.
After we went ashore at Salerno it was just a week,
When we met up with Montgomery who'd moved like a streak.
We drove northwest to Naples and east to the Adriatic Sea.
Soon all of southern Italy had been set free.
What did we gain with this invasion act?
Italy surrendered, the German southern defense had been
     cracked,
Nazi troops were diverted from being Russia bound,
And for bomber airfields we gained needed ground.
Now the south of the Nazi empire we could pound.

7. Monte Cassino

We and our Allies were driving north along Italy's mountain
spine.
The Germans had formed a defense called the Winter line.
The western part, the Gustav line, consisted of ridges and
peaks.
This was the worst for attackers. Battle outcomes looked
bleak.
From the abbey on Monte Cassino you could view all below.
Observers could direct artillery to give devastating blows.
We had mixed conclusions. The Huns were there or not.
Our commanders decided either way to blast that spot.
The monastery was built in AD 542.
Benedictine monks had occupied it since it was new.
Over 1400 tons of bombs leveled this historic place,
Because Germans could use it as an observation base.
The result of the bombardment, what more could go wrong?
We created an easily defended position that was quite strong.
It took four months and four major battles there
To dislodge the Germans from their mountain lair.
The Allies were mostly Americans and Brits,
But included eight other nations' troops in pieces and bits.
We even had Kiwis and Maoris, a unit of free Poles.
Each group fought hard in their military roles.
In May we broke through the Huns' defensive line.
The road to Rome was open, a very good sign.
One fact of which most are probably unaware,
The Nazis did something that showed they cared.
General Kesselring knew the abbey would be destroyed.
To the Vatican valuable books and paintings were convoyed.
The monks were evacuated except for a few.
The abbey was destroyed but not the religious crew.
In retrospect our having 100,000 casualties there

Was too high a price to pay, I can declare.
You should never attack a place so easily defended,
When you can bypass it and conquer land uncontended.
Besides there was no way we could invade Germany from
    below.
Too many mountains stood in the way to help our foe.
Without Monte Cassino we could have accomplished our goal.

8. Anzio

Our advance in Italy had come to a stop.
Due to the Gustav defense line on mountain tops.
Our generals decided on the Anzio beaches we'd land.
To lessen the pressure on our troops was the plan.
We were to drive inland and attack from the rear.
This required that the landing zone be kept clear.
Maybe we didn't have enough men for the attack,
Or the Huns' mobile reaction units pushed us back.
Resupply became a problem over the beach.
Ships and landing craft were targets easy to reach.
In contrast the German roads could be traveled at night.
Providing them with an advantage in the fight.
We were outnumbered and could have been pushed into the
    sea.
There was nowhere to hide, nowhere to flee.
Casualties mounted as the armies slugged it out.
Determination prevailed, and we avoided a rout.
Both sides decided it was time for a Winter break.
Lower the level of fighting for the soldiers' sake.
In May the action resumed. The German line collapsed.
We pushed forward rapidly widening the defensive gap.
On June 5 of '44 we liberated the city of Rome.
Though this was a major success, most were unaware at home.
D-Day, the long awaited invasion on the coast of France,
Dominated the news more than the Italy advance.
For the next year we kept attacking the Hun.

Pushing northward until the war was finally won.
No one benefitted from this last bit of warfare in the land of
the sun.

Chapter 8.   Pacific Submarine War

1. Sub Design
If offered a ride on a sub, most would decline.
Are we claustrophobic or do we think of the design?
When submerged, the sub needs a thick steel skin.
This holds back the pressure of the sea they're in.
They have to be buoyant in order to float.
Meaning ballast tanks fill part of the boat.
Then, diesel engines provided the power. They needed fuel.
While submerged, electric power was the rule.
Thus, batteries, generators, and motors were in need
For the propulsion system to provide underwater speed.
Subs had other equipment of most every kind.
Pumps, steering, sonar, and communications you'll find.
The result, there was not much room for the crew.
Of deprivations, there were more than a few.
They slept in shifts, three to a bunk.
There was so little space, life was better for a monk.
Then taking a shower was allowed once a week,
Since water was rationed, the conditions seem bleak.
Think of 70 men cooped up with stale air.
It's no wonder that most wouldn't want to be there.
Food was fresh only after resupply
And yet those brave souls managed to get by.
Life on a sub was far from ideal,
But they put up with it in their patriotic zeal.

2. The Sub Fleet
Submarines were named after fish during the war.
In retrospect it seems silly. Names should mean more.
We have famous people, cities, and towns.
The sub might reverse things and bring them renown.

We had about 250 serving in the Pacific.
The job they did was more than terrific.
Some 50 boats were lost fighting Japan at sea,
And 3500 men died helping keep us free.
The submariners say they're "on eternal patrol."
Their resting places can never be told.
What was accomplished for their loss so steep?
They sent 1200 merchant ships into the deep.
Japan needed material transported by ships.
The subs made sure they limited their trips.
They also rescued 380 airmen downed,
Including a future president who avoided being drowned.
That's a hell of a record for 16,000 volunteers.
Heroes each, their courage conquered any fears.

3. Torpedoes
Early in the war, torpedoes were nicknamed fish.
When they were launched, everyone made a wish.
"Please let this fish go and not abort.
No left or right, no diving or stopping short.
God willing, if you should hit the target, please go off."
Torpedoes didn't work well, so please don't scoff.
Our sub was surfaced (often the mode of attack.)
"Oh Lord, Captain, one is coming back."
No time to shoot forward, no time to dive.
If the torpedo struck, maybe none would survive.
Luck was with them on that day of woe,
The torpedo dived and passed the boat below.
Maybe a new wish should now prevail.
"If you're going to screw up, then please double fail."

4. How to Make a Friend
The boat was 250 feet down with a 20 degree roll.
The typhoon above was taking its toll.
Forty foot seas battered anything afloat.

They weren't sure if it would swamp their boat.
The captain made a decision because of need.
Their batteries were low. They couldn't make any speed.
"We have to surface, and we could use fresh air."
They were 50 miles from Japan. They would take care.
Not many ships would be about with winds so strong.
They'd run the diesels for charging, but not for long.
The boat breached, and there for all to see.
Was a one man raft in the sub's lee.
It was a downed pilot with his life about gone.
He couldn't help himself with the approach of dawn.
Two volunteers took ropes and tied them about their waists.
They'd swim and pull the raft with the greatest haste.
It seems God was with the pilot twice that day.
A wave picked him, his raft, and the sailors without delay,
And dropped them on the deck surprising all.
Strange that such could happen in the middle of a squall.
All aboard that sub survived the war.
Pilot and rescuers were friends forever more.

5. Submariner's Trick

The new ensign hadn't gotten his sea legs yet.
Given some time, he'd be a good officer I'd bet.
He got the job of establishing the boat's trim.
Keeping it level was up to him.
This is not too hard when the boat's under way.
Forward inertia and dive planes help, you could say.
Some of the crew decided to play a trick.
When the sub stopped, that's when they picked.
Several in turn walked up to the bow.
The boat tipped forward. What now?
The ensign adjusted ballast tanks for and aft.
Then the tricksters walked back. They knew their craft.
The poor ensign made adjustments again.
He hadn't noticed the movement of the men.

The sub tipped up, then it tipped down
The young officer did his job with a frown.
This kept up 'til the tricksters had duty.
The ensign was relieved. He hadn't gone fruity.
Months later they told him of their trick.
The victim it seems had the last lick.
He told the men, he wanted to say thanks.
He got needed practice from their pranks.

6. Roll
Old time subs had one advantage over the new.
This is something that really affects the crew.
The old hull was shaped for surface use.
It didn't roll so much from the wave's abuse.
The new is round, as round as can be.
Surfaced, nothing stops the roll to any degree.
So even old tars can become sick from the roll.
"Please submerge, Captain. The sea's taking its toll."

7. New Crew
It was a green crew that manned the new boat.
What was a well used word (that we can quote)?
The word was "bucket," and wonder you may.
The sub had left port, and they were under way.
Most of those submariners had never been to sea.
They joined the Navy for the adventure you'd agree.
The captain gave the command to dive.
In the back of each mind,"Will I survive?"
Boat mates looked around. Someone was grey.
The call went out "bucket," the word for the day.

8. Submarine on Patrol
They left Pearl Harbor late in the day.
The sub could travel more safely that way.
Most thought submerged was always the norm.

At night the surface was safe except in a storm.
Close to Hawaii the danger's from our own.
One flyboy mistake, and from the water they'd be blown.
They traveled northwest to the Japanese isles,
And took up station and waited awhile.
The waiting was hard in the sub's cramped space.
Some of the young wondered, "Why this place?"
Soon they learned the mission for the sub.
The sonar detected passing ships up above.
Japan needed the materials transported by sea.
Sink the ships bringing supplies, was the sub's decree.
They raised periscope and took careful aim.
A spread of torpedoes soon ended the game.
This worked fine until the fateful day.
A destroyer quietly waited, then got under way.
The sub dived as fast as it could.
Depth charges exploded right where it stood.
The men died quickly as the sub sank.
Their bodies were crushed independent of rank.
Though these sailors' graves will never be found,
We all know their strategic mission was sound.
Japan was starving for material at war's end.
The submarine force was the cause of this trend.
They died heroes doing more than their share.
Now on eternal patrol, they have our prayers.

Chapter 9.   Aircraft and Carriers

1. PBY Catalina
It was a patrol type plane, a flying boat.
Its main advantage was that it could float.
This meant it could land anywhere at sea
If the waves weren't too high or there was a lee.
They named it the Catalina, maybe for the isles.
Some sailors called it the "Cat or Dumbo," bringing smiles.
Its wings were up high with two engines there.
This avoided damage from water splashed in the air.
Machine guns provided some protection from air attack.
These were placed on each side halfway back.
They mounted bombs, torpedoes, or depth charges below
    each wing.
This didn't work so well, at the time the usual thing.
But these were good scout planes, they could stay up long.
They had radar to help spot targets with less to go wrong.
Cats could deliver cargo to inaccessible spots.
They rescued pilots. At sea they were just dots.
Slow, lumbering, but they won't be forgotten.

2. P-38 Lightning
"Ach, here they come. Get off the road."
"But there's a ditch. We'll lose our load."
"If they hit us, we'll be done. You've got my word.
Crashing is better. You don't escape that bird."
The Germans called the fighters "Jabos*" in the battle for
    France.
The enemy couldn't move supplies in daylight or slow our
    advance.
The P-38 was a main line fighter of the Army Air Corps.
In Europe and the Pacific it helped shorten the war.

We wanted a long range fighter with a one man crew.
It should be fast and fly at high altitude too.
In the late thirties Lockheed created an unusual design.
It didn't look like a fighter as we would define.
It had two engines. To the tail there were two booms.
A center nacelle provided a cockpit. For armorment there was
    room.
It was developed by Kelly Johnson's design team.
Later came the U-2 and SR-71. They were geniuses it seems.
In '39 the P-38 set a cross country record for speed.
The range was unusual for a plane of this breed.
It's max velocity was 443 miles per hour.
It could fly up to 44,000 feet with its power.
These greatly surpassed the government's desires.
Our Allies, the British, became the first buyers.
They named it the Lightning, and the name stuck.
It was meant to support bombers, but there was bad luck.
British fuel was not so good at the time,
So the Lightning often didn't do well in that clime.
However, it was named the "Fork-Tailed Devil' by the Krauts
When in North Africa, the Luftwaffa it drove out.
In the Pacific it provided fighter support,
When long range was important for any escort.
It was less maneuverable than the Zero but had more power
    and speed.
It could attack from long range, a better plane it's agreed.
The P-38 mounted a cannon and four machine guns.
It could carry up to 4000 pounds for bomb runs.
Later up to ten five inch rockets could be mounted.
This all meant great ground support when it counted.
Because of tradition, for pursuit they designated "P."
Later came "F" for fighter as it should be.
*Hunter-Killers

3. F6F Hellcat

Captain David McC flew the Hellcat fighter in the Pacific.
He was the Navy's number one ace and was terrific.
The Captain shot down 34 Japs with his beloved plane.
"The Hellcat performs well. It is rugged and easy to
    maintain."
In Sept. '43 it saw action one year after its first flight.
The F6F was a souped up Wildcat and blasted Zeros on sight.
An early major action was over Tarawa, when it was done,
We had shot down 30 Jap Zeros with the loss of one.
In fact the Hellcats had a 19 to 1 ratio of kills.
Some 305 F6F pilots became aces* showing their skills.
Most Hellcats took off from carrier decks,
But Marines also flew from the atoll island specks.
Aside from aerial combat, they supported troops on the
    ground.
Along with six machine guns, they could carry a bomb load of
    2000 pounds.
Later they added six high velocity aircraft rockets (HVAR),
And a dropable gas tank extended the Hellcats usefulness by
    far.
Over 12,000 of these fighters were made by Grumman during
    the war.
They were the most used fighter. We couldn't ask for more.
*For five verified kills.

4. F4U Corsair

The Navy wanted a fighter plane with maximum speed.
The Corsair was the concept. Would it fill the need?
Max speed meant using the most powerful engine we had.
It followed that a big prop we needed to add.
With a big prop the plane had to sit high off the ground.
Thus, the landing gear struts were the longest around.
To lessen their length, the wings had to bend down.

Thus, the inverted gull wing was proposed. Was the idea
    sound?
The landing gear had to rotate to fit in the wing.
Like other Naval aircraft, folding wings were the thing.
It had to be strong to land on a carrier deck.
With these qualifications the Corsair could be a wreck.
In fact the F4U was the fastest at the time.
It performed quite well, except it couldn't land on a dime.
Naval pilots called it a "Hog" and a "Bent Wing Widow
    Maker."
For flying from a carrier the Navy wouldn't take her.
The Marines flew and landed on regular fields.
The Corsair was fine and got the high performance yield.
Finally, it was accepted for carrier use in late '44.
It turned out it performed pretty well on every score.
In aerial combat it had a kill ratio of 11 to 1.
Primarily, it was a "Mud fighter" not to coin a pun.
Besides guns, it could carry bombs and napalm tanks,
HVARs*, 11.75 inch rockets or small rockets in banks.
Lt. KW was the first Corsair ace with 21 kills in all.
He lost five himself, three in combat, two accidental.
Of all the losses of Corsairs in the war,
Accidents were the cause of 57% or more.
Chance Vought and others manufactured 12,000 Corsairs.
They were made until '52. No other fighter can compare.
*High Velocity Aircraft Rocket

5. P-47 Thunderbolt.

I'm not sure what they thought when designing this plane.
It was the heaviest prop fighter ever and thus had to strain.
Gaining altitude was a problem especially in dog fights.
So they would try to attack with the advantage of height.
The weight gave it excessive speed in a dive.
It could hit 550 miles per hour, like in overdrive.
Eight 50 caliber machine guns with 3400 rounds

Meant hitting an enemy once would sent it to the ground.
Its nicknames of T-bolt and Jug came from US personnel.
The Brits thought this meant Juggernaut, fitting just as well.
The P-47 didn't have enough range to support
Bombers flying into Germany. They needed better escort.
Even so, "Gabby" Gabreski had a record 31 kills.
Maybe it's true, "It's less the plane and more the pilot's skill."
The Thunderbolt found its niche after D-Day.
Going after ground targets, it made the Nazis pay.
It could carry 2500 pounds of bombs, plus guns,
And ten rockets to use on its attack runs.
86,000 railroad cars, 9000 locomotives, 68,000 trucks,
And armored vehicles fell like sitting ducks.
One technique was developed to get a bomb to skip.
Trains would be hidden in tunnels to give us the slip.
Skipping a bomb into the entrance destroyed the train's end
As well as obstructing the tunnel, an extra dividend.
Republic Aviation built 15,000 P-47s and more.
It was the second most produced fighter aircraft of the war.

6. P-51 Mustang

As often was the case, the British ordered our planes.
They talked to North American Aviation's engineering brains.
A contract was signed and in 1940 the P-51 flew
After only 178 days, pretty good for something brand new.
The Mustang had six 50 caliber machine guns on its wings.
It was designed for lone range, and high speed was its thing.
Primarily, the Mustang guarded our bomber fleet.
It was meant for aerial combat where it was sweet.
Later fixtures were added to wings for other loads.
Bombs and rockets used for the ground support mode.
The Mustang was one of the hunter-killer types.
The roads and rails of France were cleanly wiped.
Well after the war a friend saw the Mustang, a close view.
He said it looked like solid steel, and yet it flew.

With its Packard engine it seemed like pure power.
German pilots in their cockpits must have cowered.
We produced nearly 17,000 Mustangs during the war.
They were flown by the Royal Air Force and the Army Air
    Corps.
The Mustang was used by other countries for decades more.

7. The New Bomber
The four engine bomber was brought out to view.
Reporters were invited since this was big news.
One young man stated when he saw the machine guns,
"Why it's a flying fortress." The name stuck. It wasn't a pun.
Initially, it had five guns, but the crews wanted more.
It wound up with 13. That's how it went to war.
Except the single gun wasn't used by popular demand.
Too many gunners shot off the tail. It became unmanned.
In Europe the Flying Fortress was mostly used
Though in the Pacific theater they also cruised.
It could carry 8000 pounds of bombs in its bay.
The range was 2000 miles which was far for the day.
The Fortress' top speed was just 287 miles per hour.
Slow as can be, even with its engine power.
Boeing built almost 13,000 of the big planes.
With 45% of the bombs dropped, they were Germany's bane.
Their contribution to our war effort certainly was plain.

8. B-29 Superfortress*
The Army Air Corps needed an advanced bomber, thinking
    ahead.
In1938, the war was coming, we knew with dread.
Several manufacturers competed with their plans.
Ultimately, Boeing came up with the best across the land.
We needed a plane that could fly long range and high,
Which required a pressurized cabin so the crew wouldn't die.
The bomber should stay above any pursuit ship's flight,

Antiaircraft guns couldn't hit it even in broad daylight.
Having built the Flying Fortress, Boeing had a natural name.
Superfortress was the designation they proclaimed.
This was a complex aircraft with production problems galore.
Finally, it was accepted for service in mid '44.
The pressurized plane required a tunnel fore to aft.
The bomb bay was not pressurized in the large craft.
The B-29 flew 350 miles per hour at 40,000 feet.
With a 3000 mile range and a ten ton bomb load, it was hard
    to beat.
For defense the B-29 had eight 50 caliber guns.
Four sets of two were remotely controlled, attackers to stun.
We built 4000 Superforts during the war.
With their design experience Boeing did much more.
All our commercial jets were the encore.
After VJ day as a stunt on how long it could stay aloft,
A B-29 flew almost 8000 miles weighing 77 tons at takeoff.
*First flight, Sept. '42.

9. Aircraft Carriers

The Yorktown was a typical carrier in World War II.
Like the six others then, she was almost new.
She was steam powered, and her fuel was oil.
Four screws propelled her and made her wake boil.
She could make 32 knots when going full bore.
Concerning her technology you couldn't ask for more.
The Yorktown carried 90 aircraft and a large crew.
2200 sailors ran the ship and the planes that flew.
These were stored topside on the flight deck aft.
The hanger deck was where they repaired the craft.
Three elevators took planes between the two.
Caring for the aircraft required a majority of the crew.
Most of the carrier's top deck was flat.
Thus, "Flattop" was the nickname derived from that.
The "Island" rose up along the starboard side

And halfway back where the deck was most wide.
That's where the command post and smoke stack were,
Plus the radar, pilot ready room, and antenna gear.
She was half a modern carrier's weight at 25,000 tons.
With a 14,000 mile range she could make extended runs.
Our carrier was more than 100' wide and 825' long.
Her antiaircraft guns made her defense quite strong.
With 54 guns from 20mm Oerlikons to five inch,
She was well armed though defense wasn't a cinch.
When under attack, the carriers had some aid.
Other protective ships fired during the enemy air raid.
Carriers made a tremendous change in the war at sea.
Now it's unlikely that ships will fight with gunnery.

10. Jeep Carriers

By any other name Jeeps would be escort carriers or baby
    flattops.
They weren't meant to launch planes for most military ops.
In the Pacific war they carried reserve planes,
When the full sized carriers' stock waned.
The aircraft took off and were transferred from the Jeep
That's so the carriers their station could keep.
No need to travel to a base far away,
As the Japs did after the Coral Sea foray.
The Jeeps were poorly armed and about half length,
But compared to a carrier they didn't need the strength.
They were more quickly built and cheaper besides.
Their slow speed none should deride.
One combat mission was to escort our convoys.
No need for speed or armorment when so deployed.
Their planes could search out U-boats which they destroyed.

11. Naval Flight

With what did a naval officer have to contend?
A short runway for starters, just to the ship's end.

There were no catapults powered by steam.
To give the plane a boost, there was no other scheme.
Like any takeoff, into the wind you must fly,
So the carrier's orientation had to properly lie.
To fit more planes, their wings had to fold.
This made them heavier if truth be told.
Now after an attack far from the ship,
If you couldn't find your way, you might take a dip.
A radio beacon or radar could attract you back,
But also any enemy aircraft intent on an attack.
For landing the carrier's orientation should have the right tack.
For this the ship should have the wind from the back.
Landing of course had another problem set.
First the pitching ship was a worrisome bet.
Pitch up too much and you crash into the bow.
Pitch down and you could smash parked planes somehow.
Three cables were there to arrest your speed.
Miss the cables and a net provided for your need.
A crash landing was one way to end your ride.
Then a bulldozer stood by to push your plane over the side.
Crashing near the ship had an advantage to you.
If able, they would send a small boat to the rescue.
Of all the pilots who flew in World War II,
The bravest or craziest were of the Naval flight crew.

Chapter 10. Equipment

1. Liberty Ships

These were the standard cargo ships of the war.
Liberty ships were a British design, but there's more.
We changed the power source from coal to oil fired.
Alterations for fast construction and lower cost were desired.
A total of 17 shipyards worked on them,
Though Kaiser on the west coast was the gem.
The normal construction time was about 42 days.
The record from laying the keel to going down the ways
Was about four days and 16 hours, a publicity stunt.
"We build them faster than they sink them," a motto rather
      blunt.
Having produced over 1550, Kaiser could brag.
The other shipyards built 1200. They didn't really lag.
They relied on off site assembly of mass produced parts.
What American industry has been known for from the start.
The Liberty ship's length was about 440 feet.
Moving at 11 knots, they weren't very fleet.
They could carry enough fuel for an 11,000 mile trip.
Going to Britain and back without refueling did our ship.
With a crew of 41 and Navy men on the guns,
They made countless cross ocean runs.
To North Africa, Britain, and Russia they went,
Bringing everything that the military wanted to be sent.
In the Pacific they ranged over millions of square miles
Carrying equipment, food, ammo, and supplies by the piles.
They brought disassembled planes, tanks, tough stuff and
      frail.
The biggest items were the large engines for the rail.
There's the story that one broke loose in heavy seas,
And drove out the ships side with the greatest of ease.

How do you fasten down hundreds of tons?
I guess they learned before the war was done.
Each ship was armed with antiaircraft and a four inch gun.
The S.S.Stephen sank a Germain raider with one.
These Liberty ships supplied all our military needs.
Their civilian seamen were responsible for these deeds.
With peace, they had no use, even with their feats.
They wound up in the reserve mothball fleets.

2. Sam's PT Boat (Patrol-Torpedo)

Young Sam had volunteered early in 1942.
He chose the Navy, the best deal in his view.
Like most young men, he had never been to sea.
It seemed a great adventure. It would fit him to a tee.
He heard about PT boats, the fastest in the fleet.
They could do 40 knots which is pretty hard to beat.
After his training he was assigned to a brand new boat.
Except for the captain, none of the crew had ever been afloat.
They were ordered to the Pacific, the Japs to fight.
Their primary prey were destroyers. They'd attack at night.
Sam had never thought of one detail, not so small.
Their presence being known was the big pitfall.
All guns would be firing like it was an air attack.
There double planked mahogany hull would splinter front to
    back.
One good point is, a shattered PT boat is hard to sink.
This gave the crew some time before going in the drink.
They were near Guadalcanal, toward battle they were bound.
So many ships were sunk here, they called it Iron Bottom
    Sound.
Jap destroyers were spotted heading their way.
Then the greatest luck, a star shell made it bright as day.
The Japs had fired it mistakenly on the opposite side.
Making themselves perfect silhouettes with nowhere to hide.
The captain gave the order. Two fish fired at target one.

Then two fired at target two, and now it's time to run.
Both ships sank in order. The PT boat turned around,
More scrap metal deposited in Iron Bottom Sound.

3. The Speedy PT

Motor torpedo boats got a lot of good press.
David versus Goliath had people's interest.
At least 525 PT boats were built before and during the war.
They were shaped like speed boats. Across the water they
    tore.
Their 80 ft length seems rather big to me,
But not compared to their proposed prey at sea.
The PT boat carried torpedoes, up to four.
Its 40 knot speed allowed it to get close to score.
Of note was the rescue of General MacArthur early in the war.
He was picked up from Manila harbor's Island of Corregidor.
All the lower ranks were taken prisoner by the Japs.
The General said, "I shall return." Maybe this was claptrap.
Later in the war, a young officer commanded a PT.
The boat was rammed by a Jap destroyer you see.
The crew managed to get to an island small.
Jack Kennedy swam for help and saved them all.
Just a couple of examples of how history was made
By the wooden PT boat. Their fame won't fade.

4. Higgins Boats

Ralph joined the Army. He didn't like anything afloat.
Especially that landing craft, the Higgins boat.
In practice training in seas somewhat rough,
Ralph had lost his breakfast. That was enough.
They were going to war. Now it was for real.
He had the jitters. How lousy could you feel.?
They were about to leave their troop ship base.
The sarge had formed them up with haste.
With packs on their backs, they climbed over the rail.

Then they climbed down the nets. Grip, don't fail.
Don't get foot or hand crushed between boat and ship.
Drop at the right time. Try not to slip.
The Higgins boat was as long as, but wider than a bus.
It held a platoon of 36 men and equipment, but just.
The boat was open to the air and to the waves.
They had to bail with helmets, the boat to save.
Higgins boats were made of plywood and some steel.
They were tough, but to the troops they did not so feel.
Ralph was able to talk to the sailor in charge.
This craft could make nine knots though it looked like a
    barge.
He told of his orders if anyone fell out.
Don't stop. There would be other pick-up boats about.
However, if a soldier went into the drink.
His pack would pull him down. Like a rock he'd sink.
He had seconds to undo buckles and straps,
Or to say his prayers if he had a memory lapse.
The sailor got Ralph safely to the beach.
The ramp dropped in water, the bottom he could reach.
The boat backed off. It had to make another trip.
More men, a Jeep, and supplies from the mother ship.
Andrew Higgins produced 20,000 of his boats or more.
Through the Pacific and the European theaters, they took our
    men ashore.
Eisenhower once stated, "For us they won the war."

5. The Venerable DUKW

It's not an acronym as you'd expect it would be,
But a model name describing the technology.
They've been called "Ducks" since entering service in '43.
They travel on land and water. They're amphibious you see.
Over 21,000 were built by the manufacturer GMC.
At first the military didn't want them. How could this be?
A Coast Guard craft ran aground in a storm.

A DUKW rescued the crew, a great demo to perform.
The DUKW was built on the famous "Deuce" truck chassis.
They added a hull and prop, homely but kind of classy.
It was used to ferry supplies from ship to shore
In the European and Pacific landings for the last half of the
     war.
The Higgins boat was better for initial landings it's true,
But the DUKW could sail in, then drive right through.
When wounded were evacuated, they could use the DUKW.
They avoided reloading to boat from truck.
The DUKW had six wheel drive to get it there,
Though there was one problem of which most are unaware.
They could move in water and on land,
But going up a bank they needed rock or sand.
Nothing too steep nor muddy river banks.
This was their limitation. They weren't tanks.
In later years many have taken the DUKW tour.
The reconditioned amphibian has its allure.
Worldwide in 25 locations they're available for sure.

6. Tim the Tanker

Tim was short and a wiry type guy.
The Army chose him for tanks and here's why.
It's better that you can easily fit,
And evacuate the tank after a serious hit.
It was advisable to get out fast.
This Tim practiced. He'd never be last
The GIs called our tanks Ronsons, early in the war.
They'd always light up when the Germans made a score.
The Sherman tank was powered by gas,
There was a reason determined by the top brass.
They wanted all their vehicles fueled the same.
This made supply simpler. For the tankers it was a shame.
Later they picked diesel. It won't burn so fast.
The crew could get out, even the guy who's last.

7. The Sherman Tank

Some of the commentary on the Sherman Tank is unfair.
There were reasons for its design which I will share.*
It was a full 33 tons. This was middle weight,
Which was limited. We needed to consider it as freight.
On and off trains twice, and the same for ships,
At least for those making the European trips.
The lighter weight had four advantages over the German tank.
Our Sherman was faster and could climb steeper banks.
It could travel on softer ground, and its range was greater.
This meant refueling could be done much later.
Finally, we had a motorized turret for our gun.
The German tankers had to hand crank theirs, no fun.
However, the disadvantages were armor too thin,
A short barrel cannon that couldn't puncture the panzer's skin,
When they converted to diesel later in the war,
They mounted a long barrel cannon somewhat evening the
    score.
I should mention some facts about which we can cheer.
We produced 80,000 during the wartime years.
The tank treads, power plant, and chassis,
Were the basis for other vehicles most classy.
They were tank destroyers, bulldozers, and self propelled guns,
Tank retrievers, flame throwers, all useful against the Huns.
The Brits used the Sherman in unconventional ways.
Such as the mine clearing tank. It had chains that flayed.
Plus, there's something that very few know.
We had tank retrieval teams always on the go.
The average disabled tank was fixed in less than a day.
They were back on the line firing away.
All-in-all even with its flaws mentioned here,
The Sherman stood up better than it would appear.
*General Marshall when told, "Our tanks can't fight against
    the panzers." Reportedly said, "Not fighting head to head
    is the answer."

8. The Jeep

The Jeep was the military's all purpose "truck."
It could travel over almost any terrain and not get stuck.
In 1940, specifications were determined by the Department of
    War.
They approved 130 US auto manufacturers and more.
Bids were received in just an eleven day span.
Only 49 days were allowed for a prototype that ran.
Three companies entered the competition and were up to par.
Willys-Overland, Ford, and American Bantam Car.
Bantam had the best prototype but lost out.
In no way did they have the manufacturing clout.
In total 650,000 Jeeps were produced in the war.
Willys and Ford shared the production chore.
Why did we need so many vehicles like these?
They were the work horses everywhere overseas.
Commanders could travel widely and see the action.
The Jeep wouldn't get stuck with its four wheel traction.
Supplies could be delivered right up to the front line.
Where no other trucks could travel, they'd be fine.
Often a Jeep would pull a trailer behind
Carrying ammo or equipment, anything they had in mind.
They brought the wounded back to aid stations,
When time was important for surgery and medication.
The Jeep provided a platform for the 50 caliber gun.
They could drive up and blast away, then run.
Later the recoilless rifle, a cannon, was mounted on the Jeep.
These could be used as antitank weapons on the cheap.
Jeeps were open to the air. A canvas top kept out the rain.
For winter there were canvas sides with plastic panes.
No one seems to know how the Jeep got its name.
There are several theories, but they come out the same.
They don't know. One theory seems to fit,
The Ford model was a "GP," a good bet that's it.
After the war GIs could buy a Jeep for 50 bucks.

For farm use they could be tractors with luck.
The Jeep started many decades of popular SUVs.
Even the grill with seven slots you often see.
Who would guess after all these years, the Jeep's popularity.

9. The Deuce-and-a-Half

American factories were a marvel to see.
We were used to vehicle production you'll agree.
But we outdid ourselves with the deuce-and-a-half.
We made 500,000 on our military's behalf.
These were produced by International Harvester and GM.
The now gone Studebaker and REO were among them.
"Deuce-and-a-Half" was the nickname of the 2 ½ ton truck.
It was also the "6x6" and "Jimmy" for luck.
The Red Ball Express gave it the most fame,
But it distinguished itself wherever it came.
It brought the GIs what they needed to fight.
It delivered what was required both day and night.
Even the infantry got rides if it worked out right.

10. Radar and Sonar

Radar means <u>ra</u>dio <u>d</u>etection <u>a</u>nd <u>r</u>anging, my friend.
You can find a metallic object from a signal you send.
By metallic it's meant an electrical conductor,
And when a radio wave hits, it's a good reflector.
Radars weren't sophisticated in World War II.
Approximate distance, elevation, and azimuth was the best
    you could do.
There are disadvantages about which most are unaware.
When your target also has radar, you must take care.
If he just detects, he can "see" you,
Four times further than you can do.
Also, he can mess up your signal reflection,
With four times your power and screw up your detection.
In this case you both know an enemy is out there.

This is all you know and just not quite where.
This wasn't a problem though, back in the war,
Since radars weren't often found up in the air.
Radars were on shipboard and on dry ground.
They were used to detect aircraft that were inbound.
Sonar is a sound detection system used at sea.
It has a lot of similarities to radar you'll agree.
With this subs could detect nearby ships,
And any obstacles in their path by reflected blips.
Like radar they can be active and transmit sound,
Or be passive and just listen to the inbound.
However, there is the disadvantage, above we took note.
Sonar equipped ships could hear sound sent by a boat.
So it always has been a rule while subs are at sea,
Listen to all the sound, but be quiet as you can be.

11. The Bazooka

There was the first bazooka. This has a comical turn.
It was a musical instrument invented by Bob Burns
He was a comedian in the 1930's in the USA.
The antitank weapon looked similar you could say.
Bazooka seemed more appropriate than stove pipe.
Which is also comical but less easy to hype.
Robert Goddard did initial work during World War I.
He was the rocket scientist when research was first begun.
The Germans found one of our bazookas in '43.
They copied it. Many think it's the reverse you see.
The bazooka was a recoilless rocket and required a crew of
      two.
One aimed and fired. The second loaded on cue.
He had to stay clear because of the back blast.
If he were too close, of all things, this would be his last.
The bazooka fired HEAT rockets, but don't think
      temperature.
They were High Explosive Anti Tank for sure.

The armor piercing ability of the rocket was due
To a shaped charge which helped it burn through.
They were effective against light armor and trucks,
But against the thick armored German tank, lots of luck.
In the back the armor was thin. On the side there was the
    track.
So the bazooka man had to have the knack.
It was best to lie concealed and ambush the tank.
The good shot was when you hit it on the flank.
Compared to an artillery piece, it wasn't so hot,
But for the infantryman, it's what they had on the spot.
They'd just hope and pray they had a good shot.

12. Flamethrowers

"We need some flame. Get to the radio man."
The artillery hadn't worked according to plan.
For the bunker they would need a direct hit.
Nothing else would make the defending Japs quit.
The Marines were too close for any more rounds.
They'd have to try a flamethrower aimed into the ground.
The flame man came up carrying his pack.
At 68 pounds, it was hard on his back.
"I think that depression should be your approach line.
When you're ready, then give me a sign.
We'll pour everything we have into that slit."
This was how they'd protect him from being hit.
Flamethrowers aren't effective 'til about 65 feet.
Thus, the flame man had to get close to apply the heat.
Flamethrowers contained four gallons of gas.
Plus a nitrogen propellant to give it a blast.
With this load you didn't want to get shot.
If the fuel got hit, it could get pretty hot.
The flame man's luck held again that day,
He shot flaming gas. Now those Japs would pay.
There were two ways the fire could cause death.

The target was incinerated or from a lack of breath.
Flaming gas burns pretty hot,
And it uses up all the air you've got.
Later in the war they had the flame throwing tank.
It had longer range and was safer to be perfectly frank.
Some may say it's pretty cruel to kill by fire.
Do you choose this quick death or a slow one more dire?

13. Napalm

"Sarge, do they know where to place that smoke?'
"Yeah, and they better be accurate. This is no joke."
The cannister was dropped by the spotter plane on recon.
It marked the Jap bunkers just like a beacon.
"Here come the fighters. They're right on the ball.
There go the fire bombs, tumbling as they fall.
Damn Japs don't have a chance in that burning hell.
They could have surrendered. It's just as well."
The napalm as a weapon had quite a yield.
Its fire covered the area of a football field.
Napalm, or gelled gas, was made to burn slow.
This was so it would seep into places down low.
The Marines it's said, added charcoal to the mix.
An even longer burning fire was the result of this mix.
The obvious effect of napalm was the fire,
But carbon monoxide and suffocation also caused you to
    expire.
Sometimes the Japs would surrender to avoid a fiery death.
When ordinarily they would fight to the very last breath.
Napalm was used to fire bomb cities as well.
Sherman didn't know the half of it when he said, "War is hell."

14. The Hand Grenade

Each infantry man carried a grenade or two.
They were called "frag" grenades and pineapples too.
This was because of the shape. The outside was grooved.

Which distributed the fragments. The grip was improved.
The Mark 2 model was developed in World War I.
It was reliable and often took the place of a gun.
The GI could toss it safely while in a fire fight,
And the enemy would be hit though out of sight.
The grenade had a pin which you pulled to arm.
You squeezed the lever closed. It could do you no harm.
After letting go, there was a four second wait.
If you didn't throw it, death was your fate.
Some brave opponents would throw the grenade back.
They needed quick reactions or a mental lack.
Since the iron grenade weighted 1.3 pounds,
A straight arm throw was best it was found.
It was claimed that our soldiers had a better aim,
Because of playing baseball and other throwing games.
The Germans had a grenade with a handle rod.
To the GIs it was a potato masher. It looked odd.
If in the open, you ran forward, then threw, then fell.
The Russians trained their troops to only run and yell.
They had to hope their enemy didn't shoot so well.

15. The M1 Garand Rifle

"The greatest battle implement ever developed," Patton's
    quote.
Given a choice, most Infantry and Marines also would so vote.
This rifle was the standard for two decades or more.
The Grunts' best friend as they went off to war.
A semi-automatic, it replaced the '03 Springfield single shot.
Every time it had to be reloaded whether you liked it or not.
The Brit, the German, the Italian and also the Jap
Relied on the bolt action and found out it was crap.
When fighting against us, they had some catching up to do.
Some reequipped with weapons whose designs were new.
The standard M1 was 43.5 inches long and weighed 9.5
    pounds.

It fired 30.06 ammo from a clip holding eight rounds.
One problem that made the GIs feel pretty dumb,
If you changed the clip carelessly, you'd get the M1 thumb.
The muzzle velocity was 2800 ft/sec, the range a quarter mile.
This combination meant just a yard drop for the projectile.
Mostly in the Springfield plant, we produced six million M1s,
All standard except the carbine and sniper model guns.
There was a choice of leather or canvas sling,
Four types of bayonets and a grenade launching thing.
The M1 could be disassembled (field stripped) with no tools.
The men were trained to do this in the dark, the rules.
They always treated their rifles well. They weren't fools

16. The E-Tool

When you're an infantryman and the shells begin to fall.
You want to disappear or at least become pretty small.
So soldiers need a personal shovel to dig that hole.
More than one wished he could dig like a mole.
That's why the Army invented the entrenching tool.
They wanted light weight and folding. That was the rule.
The latest model could double as a pick and a hoe.
As a weapon, compared to a rifle butt, it gave a better blow.
In North Africa the troops learned how to dig in.
A fox hole was better if you wanted to save your skin.
Some troops dug slit trenches in the rocky soil.
These weren't deep enough the German tanks to foil.
The Nazis would drive over the trench and make a right angle
    turn.
This would crush the entrenched GIs, a lesson to learn.
So the E-tool was meant to save your skin.
Dig a properly deep fox hole to hide in.

Chapter 11. European Air War

1. The B-17 Flying Fortress
Could we make it work? The philosophy was sound.
Bomb the Nazi's factories right down to the ground.
Primarily, we wanted to go after the aircraft production.
Having control of the air would cut our invasion's destruction.
No one wanted to have our new landing under air attack.
Reduce their production and losses couldn't be gotten back.
We made a deal with the Brits. They'd bomb at night.
We'd do the daytime raids with targets in sight.
The B-17 would form our primary bomber fleet.
It was felt with 13 guns, you could down any fighter you'd
    meet.
Flying in formation meant you could defend each other.
You would fight for yourself and also your brother.
However, while flying straight you could be hit by flak.
There was no easy way for the B-17 to attack.
In raids by hundreds of planes in '43
Losses often hit 25 percent, too much all agreed.
In several raids the Luftwaffe put up 300 planes.
Concluding we needed fighter escorts took no brains.
Finally, with long range fighters, losses dropped to seven
    percent.
They could escort the bombers wherever they went.
Still with all the losses of the entire war,
The most of any group were the fliers of the Army Air Corps.*
There was certainly opportunity for heroism flying over the
    Hun,
And 17 Medal of Honor awards by the fliers were won.
If a plane were going down, the pilot kept it flying straight,
So the other nine crewmen could evacuate.
The Fortress was tough, the flight crews agreed.

Let me quote an accolade from this brave breed.
"The plane can be cut and slashed... by enemy fire
And still bring its crew home," said this flier.
Maybe it was inanimate, but its soul we admire.
*Actually, in June 1941 it became the Army Air Force

2. Down in Flames

"Captain, we have two Krauts coming in about six o'clock."
"Hold your fire. Not you, Shorty. Make sure you have a good
    shot."
Shorty was the tail gunner. His job required limited size.
He was the gunner most likely to bag a prize.
The Germans had more time on target attacking from the rear.
However, this sector gave Shorty a shot that was clear.
(The bottom, front and tail gunners had clear fields of fire.
The other three might hit wing and tail with results most
    dire.)
The lead German started blasting and Shorty let her rip.
He caught the bastard, and its nose dipped.
Smoke billowed, and the fighter dived to its end.
The tail gun was quiet. It was also curtains for their friend.
The second fighter passed near, its guns blazing away.
Three turrets responded and ruined his day.
Two Nazis down, but the bomber took their sting.
"Captain, engines three and four are on fire. We lost part of
    the wing."
"Damn, there's no way we'll get back to base.
I can't control this old gal. Lord, help us with your grace.
Sam get back to the tail. See if Shorty's alive.
Leave the bombs alone. I'll try a shallow dive.
You guys are going to bailout, like it or not.
I'll do my damnedest to give you a good shot."
"But Captain, the crew will survive. What about you?"
"Sarge, do what I say. I order you to."
More than one pilot earned a Medal of Honor this way.

He kept the plane stable. His crew lived for another day.

3. Gary the Pilot
Gary joined up right after high school.
Seventeen is kind of young for the volunteer pool.
He was short of stature but smart enough.
Thus, the Army Air Corps figured he had the right stuff.
After his induction and the normal basic training drill,
They aimed him for flight school. Did he have the skill?
Gary didn't wash out since he worked rather hard.
Rated to fly multi-engine aircraft was his reward.
Gary trained on the B-17 bomber then.
The famed Flying Fortress had a crew of ten.
They flew to England to join the air fleet.
The Army Air Corps had a job to complete.
Their mission was to stop German arms production.
They were to bomb factories to utter destruction.
The Americans flew over the targets by day.
At night our fires guided the Brits along the way.
Gary had tremendous luck and certainly the skill.
He completed 25 missions not getting killed.
He was due to transfer back to the States.
But extra missions kept extending those dates.
Their plane had taken many hits from flak,
But always remained air worthy 'til they got back.
Then the worst that could happen in fact did.
The plane lost most power, God forbid.
No one wanted to parachute. They'd ride it in.
Maybe Gary could start another engine. Let the prayers begin.
Luck was with them as they coasted down.
Gary made a dead stick landing on the ground.
A farmer's plowed field was lined up just right.
This was the perfect spot to end their flight,
And the extra bonus for pilot and crew.
They were in Belgium, behind our lines too.

Maybe if Gary had been transferred to the States,
The crew would be knocking on the pearly gates.
This one time they didn't get the fickle finger of fate.

4. Johnny the Gunner

The B-17 tail gunner's turret was a pretty tight spot.
So they left their parachutes where they wouldn't be forgot.
Johnny was the first defense for an attack from the back.
He also was most likely to get hit from that attack.
They were over Germany when the fighters appeared.
Their cannons blasted holes as they neared.
The plane was on fire. Suddenly Johnny was free.
He was blown out, pretty bad you'd agree.
He tumbled about as the cold wind blasted him.
Reaching terminal velocity, it looked pretty grim.
Now after the first hundred feet or so,
It doesn't matter how far you go.
Johnny fell 10,000 feet it was later found.
There was time to think, a minute to hit the ground.
He was over a forested area with fir trees tall.
Johnny snapped branches going down. This broke his fall.
After he hit the round, he was rather sore,
But there were no broken bones nor any gore.
Later he was picked up by a German patrol.
They wouldn't believe the story he told.
He finished his service as a prisoner of war.
Johnny has the unbroken record in our lore
For the no parachute distance fallen survivor score.

5. New Friends

"What's the matter here? I've been on the base four days.
Nobody's friendly, no beer at the shack, no card games to
        play."
This new guy better make friends with other newbies.
The old timers are cool. To them he's like a booby.

Men who've been on a few missions and came back
Are buddies with their crew mates. They're like a pack.
Early on you made friends with anyone there,
But too many planes had been shot from the air.
When your dear friends have gone down in flames,
You can stop this by limiting friends or forgetting their names.
It's easier to think that ten planes were lost,
Than Pete, Jim, Murph and Slim were the cost.
Maybe then you can keep taking off on each raid.
You can bolster your courage even though you're afraid.
Those unknown guys were the price that was paid.

6. The Fighter

"He got one of us, and he's going down. Do you see a chute?
Let's get the Kraut. See how he does when we all shoot."
The German Me262 was fast, the first operational jet.
We had to develop special tactics. Ganging up was a sure bet.
The Air Corps also thought that hitting the German airfields
Would give us an advantage, a better kill yield.
Though fast, the Me262, taking off and landing was a sitting
    duck,
And many times our Mustangs had such luck.
Sometimes they'd follow the jet back to its base.
With their extra fuel supply they could continue the chase.
The bomber groups needed protection on their runs.
It was felt they could defend themselves with their guns,
But there was too much loss from enemy fire,
And our fighters didn't have the range they required.
The Mustang was deployed with an extra large fuel supply.
Dropable wing tanks were added. The range was multiplied.
They replaced the P-47 and could fly all the way in.
Hermann Goring said, "The jigs up," when they flew to
    Berlin.
The P-51 was the fastest prop plane of the war.
They could chase down the V-1 to even the score.

By war's end we had gotten over 9000 kills,
Including some 4000 picked off on the ground sitting still.
At the same time we lost 2500 of our own,
Damn good considering over 200,000 sorties were flown.
Flying the Mustang were two aces who rate their fame,
Test pilot Chuck Yeager with 12.5 kills to his name,
And George Preddy who shot down 27.5, his score.
This hero was a casualty on Christmas of '44
Helping win the Battle of the Bulge. He gave his all.
Unfortunately, friendly fire was the cause of his fall.

7. B-24 Escorts

The bombers took off. They were heading north.
Their airfields were in eastern Italy. From there they flew
  forth.
These were the biggest bombers at the time, the B-24.
They had the greatest range in the European war.
They hit targets in the south of the Nazi empire.
They could blast the factories or set them on fire.
"Where's our escort? They should be with us soon.
Keep an eye out. The rendezvous is to be around noon."
"Here they come, Captain. I see the red tails.
Here's hoping their great record won't fail."
The "Red Tails" or "Red Tailed Angels" deserved their fame.
They flew the P-51 and excelled in the aerial game.
From German fighters too many bombers had been lost.
With the Red Tails protecting them at all cost,
They could get through and drop their loads.
The bomber crews felt safe. Their appreciation flowed.
There was a story afloat that they never lost an escorted plane.
Not true, but they did damn well in the main.
Only 25 B-24 Liberators were lost while in their care.
Which was the best of any fighter group over there.
Who were these dashing pilots? Maybe you can guess.
They weren't allowed to fraternize in the officers' mess.

It was okay to keep the German fighters clear,
But a bomber pilot couldn't buy a fighter pilot a beer.
These were the Tuskegee Airmen, a real determined lot.
The all African American unit deserved every accolade they
    got.

8. Tuskegee Airmen

Wow, what a determined bunch they were.
The military's attitude was more than most could endure.
Forget the fact that of pilots we had a short supply,
And here was a group physically and mentally able to fly.
The entire government was segregated by race.
Equal treatment under the law, nowhere did it take place.
The high ranks were uniform in their racial hate.
Finally, they gave African-Americans a shot by opening the
    gate.
Maybe Eleanor Roosevelt led the way by doing what's right.
She visited their field and took a flight.
Anyway, pilots were finally trained starting in '41.
Almost a thousand had graduated when the war was done.
Since they thought no whites would serve under an officer of a
    darker hue,
All the ground crews were African-American too.
The pilots adopted "Tuskegee Airmen" as their name.
This was the Alabama training field from which they came.
Their first mission was after the North Africa fight.
They attacked a Mediterranean island solely with air might.
This was the first time in history that island defenders
Got hit by air power and decided to surrender.
With P-40s and P-47s they entered the Italian campaign.
Mostly the Airmen attacked ground targets again.
Then the P-51 Mustang arrived along with bombers to guard.
The Tuskegee Airmen hit the Nazis and hit them hard.
The Airmens' tradition was to paint each plane's tail red.

From "Red Tails" the bomber crews called them the "Red-
    tailed Angels" instead.
About 450 pilots were deployed overseas.
The ultimate cast was the death of 150 of these.
They did more than their share as all should agree.

9. Gremlins
Sometime during the war, the concept of gremlins arose.
Who first postulated their existence, no one knows.
Trouble often happened with machines especially planes.
There was no cause, no reason, nothing would explain.
Perhaps the engine would stall but later be okay.
The radio went dead. The controls would cause dismay.
Maybe gremlins were goblins or fairies of a special type
Who like to chew on wires or find parts they could swipe.
Some pilots swore they saw a gremlin riding on a wing.
It would give an evil grin, a devilish type of thing.
Probably the pilot was flying high where the air is thin.
Lack of oxygen caused hallucinations or something akin.
With better equipment and thorough maintenance tests,
The gremlins lost their opportunity to be such pests.
They only live on in Disney type cartoons.
Nobody believes in them now except the naive and loons.

Chapter 12.   Central Pacific, 1943, 1944

1. Tarawa*

We started our hopping from isle to isle.

We needed bases in the Marianas in awhile.

But first the Gilberts, then the Marshalls came next.

Each island was a stepping stone. They were just specks.

Tarawa is an atoll and seemed a good start.

Its largest island is Betio, the most important part.

Betio had an airfield and defenses that would stun.

Concrete bunkers protected 14 coastal defensive guns.

Trenches connected each bunker and pill box.

Machine gun nests and 40 artillery pieces guarded beaches
    and docks.

The Jap commander bragged it would take a million men

A hundred years to conquer his island den.

We had the greatest armada to date in the war

With 12 battleships, 17 aircraft carriers and much more.

I presume our Navy expected to be challenged at sea.

We certainly had more than enough for a bombardment spree.

Landings couldn't be made on Betio's ocean side.

Our invaders came in from the lagoon during high tide.

Unfortunately, during that time of the year,

The five foot tide they hoped for never appeared.

Landing craft and Amtraks couldn't clear the reef off the
    coast.

They became beached, east targets for the Japs (remember the
    boast).

The Marines disembarked and waded 500 feet to the shore.

They were in the open, unprotected, the Japs could ask for no
    more.

When the Naval and aircraft bombardment ceased,

The 5000 Jap defenders came out. Their firing increased.

We had close naval artillery support plus the air.
The carrier planes were on call. They did more than their
    share.
Half the Amtracks were knocked out the first day.
Tanks we managed to land wound up the same way.
Gradually, we pushed forward and conquered that small spot.
The Marines lost 1000 men which seems like a lot
While 17 Jap defenders and some slave laborers didn't die.
The Japs' lack of desire to surrender is why.
They even lost 300 men in a fruitless banzai attack.
This is the type action where no one comes back.
After the fight some claimed it was too high a price to pay.
Monday morning quarterbacking is what others say.
*Nov. 20-23, 1943.

2. The Reef

"Damn it. We're wedged in here. We're stuck.
The tracks won't work. We're out of luck.
We have to get moving. Follow me out.
I hope the water's the right depth. I have doubts."
If it's shallow enough, you can move fast,
But you'll make bigger targets to blast.
Any deep spots and the guys sink and can drown.
If you get rid of your gear, you won't go down.
In any operation things can go wrong,
And the hapless Leathernecks suffer all along.
"Spread out men. Maybe the Japs are lousy shots.
I hear machine guns firing from several spots.
If you see a splash, duck under if you can.
We have to get to the beach. There's no other plan."
Some men took a bullet and sank from view.
How many were left after 500 feet, just a few.
The lieutenant called out both left and right.
Most of his buddies could no longer fight.
"Clean your weapons, men, check out your grenades.

We'll get those Jap bastards. It'll be our crusade.
Maybe vengeance is the Lord's, but I'm taking a piece.
They'll all be dead, or I will before I cease."
The beginning of the Tarawa battle didn't go so well,
But these men came through this invasion hell.
That's what Marines do. That's the story we'll always tell.

3. The Amtrack

Before the war we developed the LVT.
Landing Vehicle Tracked could travel on land and sea.
It had various names such as Alligator and Amtrack.
Later Water Buffalo showed the glamour it lacked.
Originally, it was designed to carry supplies ashore.
The Amtrack had machine guns, but of armor it needed more.
It performed best when making uncontested landings.
In the Tarawa invasion, conditions were more demanding.
The Amtrack was slow, in water only eight miles per hour.
This made an easy target with the lack of power.
Some LVTs got stuck crossing the Tarawa reef.
Treads wedged or came off. Marines didn't need the grief.
Most Amtracks were used in the Pacific war.
Each got 24 fully armed Marines ashore.
Better armor and armament came along as time went by.
However, there was no easy way. In landings men die.

4. Kwajalein*

Japan acquired Pacific Islands after World War I.
Germany had been in charge until that war was done.
The Marshalls became part of the outer defense ring for the
   Japs.
They had started fortifying early with few gaps.
Kwaj is by far the world's largest coral atoll.
Two of its isles were big enough to play a military roll.
Roi-Namur and the Island of Kwaj had air bases.

There were such facilities in several other Marshall Island
   places.
We eliminated most of their aircraft with surprise attacks.
Japan decided to pull their air arm back.
We bypassed the outpost islands going directly to Kwaj.
The two main islands received a tremendous barrage.
First we invaded several nearby atoll isles
And brought in artillery and ammo by the piles.
B-24s and naval guns bombarded the Kwaj shore.
If that wasn't enough, the artillery provided more.
Each fortification was blasted with no standing palm tree.
Virtually everything was destroyed in the shelling spree.
The Marines took Roi-Namur and the casualties were light.
Unfortunately, disaster struck during the fight.
To destroy a bunker, a demolition team tossed in a satchel
   charge.
It was a torpedo warhead magazine. The explosion was large.
It killed 20 Marines and wounded dozens more.
A hell of a mistake, but it's what happens in war.
The Army took Kwaj, the Japs soon were defeated.
The whole operation took four days to be completed.
Still in the action 370 brave souls died.
To secure the atoll for the use of our side.
The Japs lost almost 20 times this count.
Thus, justifying the tremendous bombardment amount.
*Jan. 31- Feb. 3 1944

5. Eniwetok*

We planned this invasion in the Marshall Island group.
To safeguard our men, we knocked the Japs for a loop.
We attacked their big base on the Truk Atoll.
From there they could launch attacks and patrols.
Within Eniwetok's reach, this was the only base.
So destroy it we did. We leveled the place.

The Japs expected something. They moved much of their fleet,
But left behind 65 transports and warships we could easily defeat.
Our attack was a surprise, combining surface, sub, and air.
We attacked airfields, shore installations, and ships anchored there.
Our Navy waited for any ships trying to escape to sea.
Many merchantmen loaded with troops tried to flee.
Being kindly people, we followed the rules of war.
Survivors refused rescue. We could do no more.
Most Jap aircraft were destroyed on the ground.
Some were waiting to be assembled as they were found.
Their loss was 270 aircraft destroyed beyond repair,
Some 47 ships sunk, and dead too many to declare.
Two of our ships damaged, 25 aircraft lost,
Mostly from antiaircraft fire, and 40 killed was our cost.
The battle of Eniwetok went without a hitch.
However, over 260 were killed. Invasions are always a bitch.
*Feb. 17-23, 1944.

6. Saipan*

Fifteen battleships delivered one hell of a blow.
Over 165,000 shells rained down on our foe.
Saipan is a big island, not like the coral atolls.
There's plenty of room for pillboxes and holes.
You can blast away but with limited effect.
The Marines and Army still had it hard as you'd expect.
This was the first central Pacific island with jungles dense,
Where the Japs could try their in depth defense.
More than 300 Amtracks bought 8000 Marines ashore
On the western beaches. They didn't know what was in store.
The Japs had put markers to measure gun range.
Several Amtracks were blasted by an artillery exchange.
The Marines were greeted with barbed wire and trenches.

Machine guns and artillery were part of the defenses.
Even so, by nightfall our beachhead was a half mile deep.
Jap counter attacks after dark meant nobody could sleep.
With the Marines in control, the Army landed the next day.
Soon we had 70,000 troops thrown into the fray.
Moving inland we found ground was harder to gain
Since central Saipan has mountainous terrain.
Controlling the high ground always gives defense a boost.
Casualties mounted trying to blast them from their roost.
The features of the land were named "Death Valley,"
"Hells Pocket", "Purple Heart Ridge" and "One Way Alley."
When the 11 fire support ships were out of range,
The troops methods of attack required a change.
The Japs took advantage of caves in the volcanic landscape.
They knew they would die there since there was no escape.
Their philosophy was to cause as much death as they could.
Maybe the American attackers would quit for good.
We brought up flamethrowers to burn the Japs out.
Machine gun and artillery support meant the outcome had no
      doubt.
After three weeks of hard fought battles there,
The last Jap resistence ended in a flair.
The Jap commanders all committed suicide at the end.
We took just 900 prisoners. 30,000 is what they spent.
Our losses were just ten percent of the Jap price.
Still too much for me. None should suffice.
*Jun. 15- Jul. 9 1944

7. We Were So Different

After World War I, Saipan was claimed by Japan.
Japanese immigrants settled there. Integration was the plan.
On landing we found a large, hostile civilian group.
They were afraid of us. We were the invading troops.
When our Army and Marines worked their way north,
The Jap leadership sent a cruel message forth.

The emperor expected the civilians with their last breath
To either kill themselves outright or fight to the death.
They would dishonor the emperor if taken prisoners of war.
How cruel can you get? No one could ask for more.
Some died in a banzai attack, fruitless you'll agree,
While 20,000 threw themselves from cliffs into the sea.
This didn't need to happen. A Japanese speaking GI
Managed to convince 1000 that they didn't have to die.
We set up a camp. We kept lights on all night.
This was a beacon for those who didn't want to fight.
We treated them with respect, providing shelter and food.
They weren't punished or mistreated. Kindness was our
    mood.
Contrast in your mind's eye all these dying, every women and
    man.
With a grimy Marine cradling an infant, the last of her clan.
God, why do we make war? It's not part of your plan.

8. Tinian*

Tinian is a southern neighbor of Saipan.
It was natural to invade it as part of our plan.
We needed the two islands for building our air bases.
Tinian had flat terrain uncommon in these places.
From Saipan we were able to fire artillery across the strait.
This plus the naval bombardment helped seal the Japs' fate.
We faked a landing, diverting the defenders with this trick.
The invasion was easier for the Marines, our conquest quick.
However, two of our ships sustained damage from shells.
Jap artillery made 26 hits before they were quelled.
This was the first Pacific battle where napalm was applied.
Fire bombs burned away foliage where the Japs tried to hide.
Also, gelled gasoline seeped into pillboxes and caves.
The Japs could burn or run out and be brave.
After the battle some Japs hid out 'til war's end.
Maybe they had two fears, us and their own friends.

Soon 15,000 Seabees built six long runways there.
From these the Army's B-29 aircraft took to the air.
They built camps for 50,000 men in the Army Air Corps.
This was truly a mixed effort common in the war.
*Jul. 24-Aug. 1 1944

9. The Battle of the Philippine Sea*

Go on the offensive, ordered the Japanese Naval Command.
They included land based aircraft in their plan.
Operation A-GO would start when the time was right.
Our invasion of Saipan would be where they'd fight.
The Jap combined fleet sailed to meet us there.
Aircraft on Guam Island, their attack would share.
Our subs detected their presence, thus no surprise.
We had assembled a fleet twice the Japs' size.
Admiral Spruance commanded our Task Force 58.
His worry was being drawn away by a Japanese feint.
This wasn't the case. The Japs sailed our way.
We didn't want a night battle, we preferred day.
Radar provided a tremendous advantage for our side.
Jap aircraft approaching had no place to hide.
Our F6F Hellcats first tangled with Guam's planes.
We decisively whipped them, a victory easy to attain.
Then Jap naval aircraft were launched in four attacks.
Each time with high losses, we successfully drove them back.
Only a few got through to our fleet.
Dense antiaircraft fire sent them into the deep.
The battleship South Dakota took a direct hit.
She wasn't disabled. There were casualties, but that was it.
One pilot was overheard remembering a hunting game.
"The Great Marianas Turkey Shoot," became the battle's
     name.
The next day we went on the offensive sea and air.
Two of our subs went after their carriers and got a pair.
Taking a torpedo when you're refueling your planes

Results in explosions and fires that you can't contain.
Both ships' crews fought the spreading fire,
But they didn't win and their ships expired.
Late on the second day of the battle, our planes pressed the
    attack.
We lost 20 from Jap fighters and antiaircraft flak.
With aerial torpedoes and bombs another carrier slipped
    beneath the waves.
Many other ships were damaged and two tankers went to their
    graves.
Night had fallen. Our planes returned home.
Landing on a carrier in the dark can send you into the foam.
The order went out to turn on all the lights
Give the pilots a chance to land at night.
Even so 80 planes crashed on deck or at sea.
Many were rescued in the next day or three.
The Japs never recovered. They couldn't replace their planes,
And of skilled pilots, damn few of them remained.
*June 19-20, 1944

10. Guam*
Of the "big" islands in the Marianas group, Guam was the
    third
That we needed for bases about which you have heard.
Guam had been a U.S. possession since 1898.
Its two airfields and a deep water port were great.
The Japs captured it soon after the Pearl Harbor attack.
Now it was time for us to get it back.
Unfortunately, the island was ringed with cliffs and reefs.
Of suitable landing spots, the list was brief.
The Marines made it ashore twice on the isle's west side.
Twenty Amtracks were lost. Too may Marines died.
The Army had only landing craft, the reefs they couldn't clear.
GIs had to wade, and the beach wasn't that near.
Getting supplies ashore also was pretty hard to do.

Landing craft couldn't make it. Of Amtracks there were too
  few.
By nightfall the beachhead had gained a mile in the fight.
The Japs dropped back but counterattacked at night.
They exhausted themselves this way, and after ten days
Lack of ammo and food meant fleeing in disarray.
The Japs last stand was in the north of the isle.
As in other battles, not giving up was their style.
Of 22,000 Jap troops, less than 500 surrendered.
The leadership of Japan gained nothing from Guam
  defenders.
Maybe these men could have helped in the postwar years.
Fighting for a lost cause gained them no cheers.
The Seabees built five large airfields on Guam.
These were available in the bombardment to come.
A note showing how dedicated the Japs were here,
One of their men was discovered having hid for 27 years.
*Jul. 21- Aug. 8, 1944

11. Peleliu* (Palau)

The Japanese leaders learned from the war.
Tactics were changed for defending island shores.
No more trying to stop our men early in the attack.
When the bombardment starts, keep under cover and fall
  back.
Have prepared positions. Defense in depth it was called.
When you retreat, you have other barricades or walls.
No more banzai attacks, a stupid waste of men.
Better to try infiltration at night. GIs are less alert then.
Some techniques were tried on Saipan at first.
On Palau they went further. For us it was worse.
They used more concrete. Some openings had steel doors.
Gun emplacements and block houses were connected and
  more.
Inland Palau had hundreds of limestone caves

Tunnels were created, the defenders lives to save.
For the emperor soldiers were still expected to die.
With the new order they'd kill and wound more GIs.
Stretcher bearers, they even planned to shoot.
These were easy targets which you'd expect from such brutes.
In the western Pacific there were two action plans
After Palau came the Philippines or Formosa** on the way to
    Japan.
MacArthur verses Nimitz and the Philippines was it.
In either case Palau probably should not have been hit.
The maxim "Hindsight is always 20-20" should fit.
*Sept. 15- Nov. 27 1944
**Now called Taiwan

12. The Point

The Navy thought it had done its job. Blasting the Japs to hell
Were battleships and cruisers, tons and tons of shells.
Not much can survive a 16 incher's direct hit,
But enough of the defenses survived in spite of it.
When our Amtracks approached, Japs opened the steel doors.
Artillery sank many before they reached the shore.
Marines both wounded and lucky had to wade.
Many lost their equipment in the cannonade.
They were pinned to the beach with fire from "The Point."
The Leathernecks had no time, that fortification to anoint.
The Colonel told the Captain, "Take company K forth,
And capture that position raining fire from the north."
One platoon was pinned down for nearly a day.
In a vulnerable position between fortifications they lay.
Counterattacking Japs had cut through their lines.
Conditions looked serious until a good sign.
One rifle platoon began knocking out the Jap guns.
Using smoke grenades for cover, they'd run
And sweep through each enemy position until
They knocked out six machine guns on the hill.

Finally, the 47 millimeter artillery piece fell.
Smoke helped and a grenade detonated some shells.
This wasn't the end of the story for Company K.
The Japs counterattacked over and over for more than a day.
The Marines were low on supplies, out of ammo and water.
Hand-to-hand combat drove the Japs away. It still was a
    slaughter.
We kept control of "The Point", but the cost was high.
Eighteen men were left. 157 were wounded or died.
This was the trend for the entire Palau campaign.
We had 8000 wounded and 1800 were slain.
At 34% this was the highest proportion per battle, but still,
The Japs, as usual, lost more than 98% killed.*
Was the battle worth it? One thing we can say,
It helped safeguard our bomber base from a Jap foray,
And provided another base for the Philippine attack,
Which might not have been necessary looking back.
*Some 35 Japs didn't surrender for 30 months more.
A Japanese admiral convinced them of the end of the war.
I'm sure the emperor was impressed on this score.

13. The Philippine Invasion

General MacArthur had promised, "I shall return."
The rational behind this I cannot discern.
The Philippines are farther than the Marianas from Japan.
Those islands provided bases for the bombing plan.
Thousands of Indonesian islands had been skipped.
Plus all of southeast Asia was left in the Japs' grip.
So why did we invade that Philippine land?
Was it strictly due to General MacArthur's demand.
Japan still had a strong navy but few carrier planes.
Invading could push them back toward coastal sea lanes.
We landed on the Philippine Island of Leyte in the east.
From there we could go northwest until resistance ceased.
The Japs reacted. They tried to destroy our landing force.

They sent their navy to drive us away, of course.
Nearby a major naval conflict took place.
The decisive Battle of Leyte Gulf quickened the war's pace.
The Japs managed to reinforce with supplies and men.
Leyte required several months to conquer then.
Other Philippine Islands including Luzon were won.
It was hard all the way. With Japan's surrender it was done.
The Japs wouldn't give up, especially Manila harbor forts.
We pumped diesel fuel in and set it off as a last resort.
In all, ten divisions plus five independent regiments more
Made it the biggest campaign of the Pacific war.
More Americans were involved in the Philippine advance
Than in North Africa, Italy, or southern France.
What did we gain from our Philippine foray.
Not much considering 14,000 died along the way.

14. The Photographer
I was talking to the old guy after lunch one day.
He began telling about his job back in the big fray.
It seems photographers were one of the military's needs.
I figured this was a plum job. Most would agree.
Take pictures of generals and other big shots.
Maybe take a few battle scenes but not when it's hot.
He was in the Philippine campaign near the end of the war.
Did he take the famous shot of MacArthur wading ashore?
No, but he was there. As you'd expect, it was staged.
The big man wanted the world to know he was fully engaged.
Then my photographer friend told me what they really did.
They went on recon patrols. In the jungles they hid.
They were tasked with sneaking up on camps of the Japs.
Take pictures of layouts, determine positions on maps.
Old cameras were heavy, the film on glass plates
Lugging this stuff on jungle trails, it was a heavy weight.
Who would have guessed they accompanied the Rangers,
And their craft required they face lots of dangers?

My new friend had a gain besides surviving the war.
His life time profession became photography. He desired no
   more.

15. The Last World War I Vet*
Frank Buckles didn't think 94 years ahead back then.
He tried three times to join up with the other men.
Too young, too thin, and besides he had flat feet.
The Navy and the Marines said no each time they'd meet.
Join the ambulance service, and you'll get to France.
Frank did so. He got to the war. It was his chance.
He was stationed in England 'til he became an officer's aide.
Then he got to the western front where he stayed.
Frank drove an ambulance which could be dangerous work.
An errant German shell could dive out of the murk.
Once he settled in a hospital bed. He was dog tired.
He gabbed with a buddy who by the next morning had
   expired,
The Spanish flu had sickened the man. In a few hours he died.
Frank didn't get the flu though he'd slept at the man's side.
After the war there was no VA, no vet help, no GI bill.
He attended business school and gained needed skill.
Frank worked at various jobs with a shipping line.
For the next 20 years his life was pretty fine.
Unfortunately, he was in Manila when World War II began.
Frank was taken prisoner by the invaders from Japan.
He spent 39 months in Los Banos, the prison camp.
Though he dropped to 75 pounds, he survived, our champ.
In early '45 the prisoners had an execution fear.
Two escaped to tell our troops who were near.
The 11th Airborne parachuted early in the day.
It was perfectly timed, is what you could say.
The Jap guards were doing calisthenics and had no arms.
All 2000 prisoners were rescued. None came to harm.
Frank had saved his shoes, shirt, and shorts.

He got them from his burning barracks, though not a reckless
   sort.
He just wanted to look neat when they got him out.
It was self respect. He was never broken. There was no doubt.
Frank was late to marry, but it was still for 50 years.
He had only one child. He outlived all his peers.
Frank Buckles was the very last of our first war vets.
Looking at his life, he was as tough as you get.
*Due to his World War II experience.

16. The Camp Cabantuan Raid

In central Luzon this prison camp was found.
For almost three years Americans had been in this compound.
The more able bodied had been shipped out
To be slave laborers in Japan and there about.
Some 500 remained in early '45. Guards were there too.
Part of the camp was barracks for troops passing through.
The US Army was nearing, a few days away perhaps.
The POWs all thought they would be killed by the Japs.
They also knew about the Army's approach.
They had built a clandestine radio with parts they had
   poached.
The POWs worried what would happen when they got relief,
Since they knew their captors were cruel beyond belief.
The Japs had a rule, ten prisoners would die
For each one who escaped or even tried.
They were in a quandary. Should they risk it and stay,
Or take the big chance and try to get away.
The Army had no time to hatch a good plan.
Usually, they could collect intel and train every man
For a special operation, a type of raid,
To rescue the POWs would be their crusade.
They knew from disease and malnutrition the POWs would
   be weak.
They wouldn't be able to walk. Conditions would be bleak.

A plan was put together. A 138 man Ranger troop
Would rendezvous with a 250 Filipino guerilla group.
They hiked 30 miles undetected behind the enemy's back,
On Jan. 30 they surrounded the camp for a nighttime attack.
A Black Widow night fighter flew around
Diverting the attention of the Japs on the ground.
In a 30 minute attack all hell broke loose.
Up to 1000 enemy were killed. There was no truce.
Allied casualties were, killed- one POW and two GIs,
Wounded- 20 Filipinos and four Americans. What a surprise!
For the 500 rescued POWs the raiders did provide
Ox carts carried them back to our side.
After three years confinement, like kings they should ride.
The Rangers and guerillas have well deserved pride.

17. Leyte Gulf Preliminaries

Our Third Fleet under Admiral Halsey made carrier raids
    before
The landings on the Philippine Island of Leyte's eastern
    shore.
We attacked Jap airbases on Formosa and the Ryukyu Islands.
This was to eliminate their redeployment close at hand.
In three days, after a knock-down, drag-out fight,
The Japs lost 600 planes. We eliminated their air might.
These were land based aircraft, the Jap's reserve.
Now in the Philippines defense, no new aircraft would serve.
The Jap commanders then knew they'd face an attack.
They had devised a naval maneuver that should drive us back.
If we closed their sea lanes even if the fleet survived,
It would be useless. It could no longer thrive.
Ships near Japan could get no fuel supply.
For those in the south no ammo or arms could get by.
They divided their fleet into three different parts.
The "Northern Force" was to lure us if we weren't too smart.
Their aircraft carriers devoid of aircraft would be the bait,

While Leyte would be approached through two straits.
Our subs on parol noted the approach of their Center Fleet.
This was reported. The subs sped ahead for a daylight meet.
Of the heavy cruisers, spreads of torpedoes hit three.
Two sank quickly. The third had to flee.
The "Atago" was the admiral's flag ship. He had to swim,
A bad start for the Jap navy though they rescued him.

18. The Battle of Leyte Gulf*

Four battles occurred in the Leyte Gulf or near there.
The Japs had divided their fleet to catch us unaware.
At Leyte they wanted to blast our landing force,
And decisively smash our navy in due course.
They counted on their land based aircraft nearby.
From the Philippine Islands' air bases they could fly.
Our carrier planes spotted the Center Force drawing near.
Many waves of our aircraft attacked, our mission clear.
We went after the big ships, their battleships were tough.
There was damage, but it often was not enough.
One battleship took eight torpedoes and 20 bombs.
It finally capsized and quickly went down.
The air battle continued with raids on Jap airfields
Their planes attacked us though their fate was sealed.
Most were shot down. One of our aces bagged nine.
However, a Jap got through our defensive line.
He hit a light carrier, the "Princeton," a lucky shot.
This one bomb caused a fire exceptionally hot.
She sank quickly when her magazine blew.
This damaged another ship trying to help her crew.
When the Jap fleet reversed course, Admiral Halsey thought
They were too damaged, a safe harbor they sought.
He sent part of his fleet for fuel and to rearm,
And part to confront the Northern Force, no cause for alarm.
Meanwhile that night, the Japs reversed course again.
All but two of their ships were still battle worthy then.

They plowed eastward in the cover of dark.
Our patrol planes didn't observe their mark.
Would this spell disaster due to our mistake?
Often in war victory is determined by a twist of fate.
*Oct. 23-26, 1944

19. The Battle of Surigao Strait
The Southern Force approached the Surigao Strait.
They had arrived in three components, two parts late.
Strict radio silence meant they couldn't keep together.
This was to be a night battle, for us nothing better.
We had six battleships, five recovered from the Pearl Harbor
　　attack.
This was a good chance for the big payback.
Also, we had eight cruisers, 28 destroyers, and 39 PTs.
The Japs had no idea what they faced from all these.
The PT boats were first to spot the Jap ships.
They made torpedo attacks. The result was zip.
Our destroyers lined the strait, both sides.
The Japs had to run the gauntlet with nowhere to hide.
The destroyers fired more torpedoes with effect.
Our superior radars allowed us the Japs to detect.
With background clutter their radar couldn't spot us.
Unlike the open sea, for us the surrounding islands were a
　　plus.
The Japs couldn't respond when our big ships fired.
Their superior night fighting advantage had expired.
Surviving Jap ships turned and tried to flee.
Stragglers were attacked by aircraft, subs and PTs.
Battleship verses battleship, the ultimate in naval war
Ended in this Pacific battle. It would happen no more.

20. The Battle off Samar Island
Admiral Halsey had moved north not expecting the worst.
He was unaware that the Jap Center Force reversed course.

The Japs moved at night coming toward the Leyte beach.
If they got there, all our landing forces would be within reach.
Sixteen light carriers had been left behind.
With only a few destroyers, we were in a bind.
When we became aware of the Japs coming near,
The fleet commander gave the order, the decks to clear.
"Take off with any ordinance you have onboard.
Even if you're unarmed, go attack. Help us, Dear Lord.
If you have no bomb, then still make that bomb run.
Maybe another plane will get in while you're under the gun."
He then commanded his ships to head for a rain squall,
While the destroyers laid down a smoke screen to hide them
     all.
One of our destroyers, its captain acting on his own,
Charged at flank speed toward the Japs all alone.
The commander saw this and ordered three more.
This was one of the bravest actions of the war.
The attacking destroyers laid down a torpedo spread,
Causing the Jap ships to change course up ahead.
We received fire with this suicidal charge
From the Jap fleet, ships small and large.
Meanwhile the carriers fled south under Jap fire.
All were damaged, but only one expired.
The Jap commander decided due to unrelenting air attacks,
That he had stumbled on a major carrier group and so turned
     back.
The day was saved. Of luck and heroism there was no lack.

21. The Final Action
The Jap Northern Force was meant to draw our fleet away.
We successfully attacked them with no delay.
Our naval air flew over 500 sorties in all
Sinking their four carriers and destroying planes in the brawl.
Halsey received word of the attack on our light carrier fleet,
And sent part of his force south this challenge to meet.

They were too late to help out in any event,
And weren't needed anyway since the Central Force went.
Summing up, Leyte Gulf was the biggest naval battle ever.
The Japs lost 28 ships even with their plan most clever.
Of light carriers and destroyers, we lost three each.
The St. Lo, a carrier, was the first ship the Kamikaze reached.
This was the introduction to what was in store,
When we approached the home island's shore.
The Jap navy, however, was but a little threat.
They stayed in port since no fuel they could get.

Chapter 13. Normandy Invasion

1. Ready for the Big Day

For two and a half years we had been getting ready,
Even though fighting in the south had been steady.
Everyone knew the Alps, we'd never push past.
A landing in France would happen at last.
Our industrial output had doubled and doubled and doubled
    again.
A large part went to England to support our men.
Some folks thought the island would sink to its doom.
With military equipment, there was little free room.
Our GIs had trained to learn all of war's craft.
They filled the British Isles from for to aft.
The locals objected, "They're overpaid, oversexed, and over
    here."
Americans didn't like things British especially warm beer.
Fifty divisions were ready to attack the Atlantic wall.
Only two had seen action, the greenest army of all.
Young men have this invincible feeling. It won't happen to me.
Maybe this is better when attacking from the sea.
They don't know the many ways you can get wounded or die.
They're most likely to charge with a battle cry.
We were ready. We had the men. We had the stuff.
We had the plans, but was it enough?
In such operations it comes down to one basic fact.
How does an army of teens and twenty somethings react?
Do enough charge forward as they are expected to act?

2. Where to Land and When

When planning the invasion of Europe from the sea,
Careful consideration had to be made you'll agree.
You study every aspect to determine each need.

This couldn't fail if the Continent was going to be freed.
You need a continuous stretch of beach.
This must be close enough for fighters to reach.
There must be enough room for five divisions to land.
High tide can't completely cover the sand.
There should be a mild slope for LSTs to unload.
Nearby for free movement, you need interconnecting roads.
In the landing zone there can't be a fortified port.
Nearby for our use there should be an appropriate sort.
The landing shouldn't be too far from the German border.
The Normandy beach of Calvados was made to order.
To study the French coast, the Brits made a plea.
Please send in picture post cards from vacations by the sea.
Ten million was the response. It would have been a confusing
    mess,
But a study of the pictures helped more than you can guess.
Would the beach support a tank? Would it get mired?
Frog men went ashore at night. Data was acquired.
They approached the coast in a miniature type sub.
The whole operation depended on this. That's the rub.
To determine fortifications, we relied on the French
    Resistance.
They found gun sizes, concrete thickness, location and
    distance.
One courier was a boy with a great memory and blind.
He could go where he wanted. The Germans didn't mind.
Information was gathered and reported to the Brits
By radio in code or carrier pigeons with special message kits.
We had the where but how about the whens.
Warm weather was best, the storms less intense.
Low tide, then rising, for a landing at dawn.
This, so grounded landing craft would float and be gone.
A half moon for the paratroops would provide enough light.
The fifth of June on all accounts was just right.
If the weather was bad, we could postpone one night.

3. The Fake Out

The Brits were masters of deception and intrigue.
The Germans especially were out of their league.
Early on our Allies captured "Enigma", the German coding
    machine.
Together with the "Ultra" intercept, information we'd glean.
We were able to read radio messages, but we had to take care.
They weren't to know of our capability there.
Also, the Germans had planted spies in the British Isles.
These were captured early and turned for our wiles.
The spies still transmitted information. It was always true,
But too late to be of use or of little significance if new.
The most important use of all this disinformation
Was to encourage the Germans to be wrong in their
    estimation.
We created a fictitious First Army with plywood planes and
    rubber tanks.
General Patton who had no command was in on this prank.
In Scotland fake radio signals discussed military supply.
Stuff that a large body of troops needed to get by.
These ruses were meant to convince the Hun of two things.
We planned to attack Norway and at Pas-De-Calais that
    spring.
Also, the Germans were led to believe we had a great force
That was twice as big as was used in due course.
The deception meant on Normandy beach we wouldn't land.
After, they were to believe that this was a deception planned.
The Germans already had convinced themselves that we'd
    land at Calais.
This was confirmed with our Ultra intercept every day.
Churchill summed up, "Never in military history," in his view
"Had so many been immobilized by so few."

4. The Gathering

From all over Great Britain men and material came.

Scotland, Northern Ireland, and Wales, by boat and train.
Every port, every river and stream on England's south side
Was filled with landing craft waiting for the big ride.
Fields were overloaded with vehicles of every sort.
Piles of whatever the troops could use surrounded each port.
The men separated by unit, were quartered in tents.
The big day was coming. Feelings were intense.
Once in their camps very few were allowed to leave.
They meant to keep the operation secret, you better believe.
Some had trained for more than two years.
Now was the time for unit planning and briefing of all peers.
Officers and NCOs studied mock ups of the beach,
The terrain and defenses they would have to breach.
Never had a military operation been so thoroughly planned,
Than this invasion from the English Channel to land.
Strangely enough the Germans didn't interfere too much.
A couple of bombers and recon planes flew over and such.
Two E-boats (equivalent to a PT) fired on a practice run.
They sank two LSTs* disastrously before they were done.
They seemed well aware of our buildup for attack.
Maybe they couldn't respond was why they held back.
This was the same when our armada approached the shore.
One would think they'd resist with a lot more.
As the fateful day approached, we began loading the ships.
Each had to have the right unit and be properly equipped.
All the landing craft and transports met the warships at sea.
They each had orders and knew where they should be.
Over 2700 ships and boats were in the fleet
Plus 2600 Higgins boats loaded on LSTs.
The plan included paratroops arriving at night,
Bombing by the Brits in the dark and American at first light.
The beach and fortifications would be blasted with naval
        guns.
Some landing craft would fire rockets on their approach runs.

The D-Day landing was the most complex operation in the history of war.
Would it be enough to break through on the Normandy shore?
*LST or Landing Ship Tank

5. First Contact

The Dakotas approached their assigned drop zones.
There were over 800 planes, but they all felt alone.
Each was an easy target flying low and slow.
German antiaircraft fire blasted up from below.
Sixteen paratroopers thought it the greatest fireworks display,
Until they heard impacts on the wings creating dismay.
Machine gun bullets penetrated the fuselage of the plane.
Men instinctively covered their crotches to avoid the pain.
The door was open. The red light was lit.
Lieutenant Bob was ready until he was hit.
He was knocked to the floor but rose again.
As he jumped out the door he called, "Follow me men."
He could have held back to seek medical aid.
That was not his style. It was not how he was made.
Lieutenant Bob died sometime before he hit the ground.
His men searched until his body was found.
He was the first American officer to die on D-Day.
Bob was outstanding, a leader of men you could say.
Like the rest, he had trained for over two years.
He had mastered every aspect of fighting in his army career.
The troops loved and respected him. He was a good guy.
He represented the best the country had. Why'd he have to die?
That's the question we'll always have. Why, God, why?

6. Airborne Attack

From many airfields on that dark night they stole.
The base of the Cotentin peninsula was their goal.
Two divisions of paratroops flew, the 82nd and 101st.

They would meet clouds ahead, for navigation the worst.
They flew in formation, separation distance about 100 feet.
Flying transports in daylight, it would be close for this fleet.
There were beacons in the channel to provide a guide.
Path finders would mark drop zones on the far side.
Pilots kept track of each other with tiny lights,
Radio silence was mandatory even in the dark of night.
They were to fly parallel to the landing coast coming in from
    the west.
Considering navigation problems and terrain, this was the
    best.
Unfortunately, Murphy's Law seems to screw up the best
    plans.
The air armada flew into a cloud bank approaching land.
To avoid air collisions the planes gradually spread.
Making matters worse, the path finders were lost up ahead.
Their passage alerted German antiaircraft gun crews.
Who filled the sky with bullets and flak, pretty bad news.
Some pilots gained altitude, some dropped to the deck
Trying not to be shot down and avoiding a wreck.
Only one of 20 path finders had found the right spot.
Most approaching planes dropped their troops without being
    shot,
But the men were dropped all over the countryside.
Some landed in water. They couldn't get free and so they died.
Very few found their units. Each man felt alone.
They joined up with whoever they met in their drop zone.
Each man had a clicker. He would give one click.
The response was two. You should answer quick.
The most odd grouping consisted of officers of high rank.
They came upon a few enlisted men, fortunately all Yanks.
"Never were so few led by so many in war."
Was the quip that has entered our military lore.
This whole fiasco seemed to be the worst news,
But an unplanned benefit came from these dispersed crews.

The Germans couldn't figure what was going on
Because our troops cut every phone line they came upon.

7. D-Day Aircraft Attack

Transports had dropped the airborne troops inland.
Next the heavy bombers aimed their loads at the sand.
Unfortunately, most bombs landed two or three miles away.
Doing absolutely nothing for the invading men that day.
They hoped to crater the beach for the GIs.
Pre-dug foxholes weren't there to our surprise.
Next the B-26 Marauders came in low and fast.
Their job, pinpoint bombing, the fortifications to blast.
They did okay at Utah beach, at Omaha not so well.
Reinforced concrete requires precise hits to blow it to hell.
Coming in low the antiaircraft guns had their way.
At 600 feet there's no time to evacuate. On board you stay.
Ejection seats hadn't been invented yet.
Jumping from the plane's side door was your best bet.
The Marauders also hit the inland town of Carentan.
Bottling up an elite German unit was the plan.
They successfully cratered all the roads in and out.
If the Germans wanted to fight, they'd walk or wait about.
Meanwhile, over 5000 fighters patrolled the skies,
Protecting the fleet from any Luftwaffe surprise.
All the fighter jocks were missing the action.
Previously, they'd eliminated the Luftwaffe with total
    satisfaction.
What planes the Germans had left had fled from France,
Probably for the defense of the Fatherland to enhance.

8. The Invading Fleet

The Germans had sown the Channel with mines.
These had restricted shipping of most kinds.
With our large fleet steaming to the coast of France,
We needed to eliminate sinking from mines by chance.

Over 250 mine sweepers cleared the way,
And our ships crossed the Channel safely that day.
Well before dawn we arrived off the coast.
The LCTs* were closest of the mighty host.
The battleships and cruisers were in line in back.
At the proper time after the planes finished their attack,
They started shelling the fortifications along the beach.
You'd expect nothing would survive within the gun's reach.
We had just three battleships firing at the shore.
From our experience in the Pacific we could have used more.
Some fortifications were hardly touched by the shells,
Though the defenders felt it was some kind of hell.
The LCTs started in, each carrying four DD tanks.**
These had big canvas float bags. Unfortunately, too many
     sank.
They were launched three miles out at sea.
Their floats often broke the minute they were set free.
One LCT captain saw this disastrous crime,
Where tank crews drowned. There was no escape time.
He sailed his LCT in close to the beach.
His tanks drove off and charged into the breach.
The Higgins boats were in line after the LCTs.
These carried assault troops in from the sea.
Transports and LSTs carried more army platoons
Some LSTs pulled Rhino ferries built on pontoons.
Each could carry up to 42 vehicles on its deck,
A cheap way to carry stuff but definitely low tech.
Destroyers cruised around guarding all those afloat.
We only lost one ship to a torpedo from a German E-boat.
Several small craft hit mines near the shore.
A pretty successful crossing. You could ask for little more.
*Landing Craft Tank.
**For dual drive, one being a propeller.

9. Airborne on the Ground

The paratroop attack had one purpose to be frank.
They were dropped on the Cotentin to protect our right flank.
The Army's 4th Division would land on Utah beach,
It was good, but solid ground beyond would be hard to reach.
From a nearby river the Germans had flooded that spot
Four causeways in from the beach are not a lot.
The airborne were to secure the inland causeway ends.
Plus, eliminate several gun emplacements for their friends.
They were to blow some bridges, save the rest.
Capturing a special crossroad town was their quest.
This would help seal off the Germans from resupply,
So we could capture the port of Cherbourg by and by.
The poor paratroopers had been dropped here and there.
They each had personal equipment with no ammo to spare.
Radios, explosives, heavy weapons just couldn't be found.
Some decided bravery and aggression would gain them
       ground.
In small groups men found the enemy and fought,
But by dawn concerning goals, their efforts meant naught.
With light more groups gathered together in force.
Until a group of 2500 coalesced in due course.
By skill, determination, and old fashion guts.
They were able to safeguard the Utah landing, but just.
All objectives had been reached as night fell.
Glider troops reinforced them limiting their hell.
Their stories are too much for this poet to tell.
Please read further. Several books excel.

10. Utah Beach*

Of five beaches for landing, Utah was on the west.
As it turned out, conditions there were the best.
The Marauders had done excellent bombing runs,
Pounding the fortifications manned by the Huns.
However, the plans for attack just didn't work out.

Landing order was mixed. The outcome was in doubt.
The DD tanks were too slow to be first in line.
The Higgins boats passed them, not a good sign.
Men landed without the protection of the tanks.
Fortunately, enemy fire was light against our ranks.
General Teddy Roosevelt was on the first craft to land.
They were miles to the left of their destination as planned.**
Teddy made a decision. The meaning was clear.
The quote, "We'll start the war from right here."
The men were unfamiliar with the defenses on the shore.
This was not the beach they had planned for.
The defenders fighting skills were the Wehrmacht's least.
Many were impressed in Poland and Russia to the east.
Some killed the German sargeant who was in charge,
Then surrendered, some in groups quite large.
They told us the location of minefields nearby.
Even then the "Bouncing Betties***" caused many to die.
When the demolition teams arrived, they blasted obstacles on
    the beaches.
For the landing craft they cleared eight 50 foot breaches.
There were no mine detectors for the first groups ashore.
They probed with bayonets. No one could ask for more.
Ultimately, the demo teams found 15,000 mines.
The Seabees and combat engineer's bravery shines.
By nightfall we had landed 1700 vehicles and 20,000 men.
We had made contact with both airborne divisions by then.
The cost was 175 men wounded or killed,
Of all the Normandy beaches the least blood spilled.
*June 6, 1944.
**Due to smoke and currents.
***Mines that sprang up to explode at knee height or above.

11. A Quick Stop

B company of the 29th Division approached the shore with
    care.

Their coxswain cried out, "We can't go in there."
The captain pulled his 0.45, "You'll go straight in."
The coxswain did, just about scared out of his skin.
B company disembarked as the bullets rained down.
Only one reached the beach not wounded, killed, or drowned.
Private H took a bullet through his helmet with little harm.
Another killing shot hit his rifle carried at port arms.
Maybe the Star of David protected him from the attack.
This plus "The Bronx, New York" was painted on his back.
He saw the glint of a helmet up on the bluff.
He got off one shot. His broken rifle wasn't strong enough.
An 88 shell exploded and the shrapnel flew.
His cheek and jaw were shattered, his lip cut in two.
The tide was coming in. He got a leg wound then,
But managed to get to the sea wall with the other men.
He tried to pull a medic down from harm's way.
"You're injured. When I'm wounded, you can have your day."
Private H got shot the fifth time in the firing spree
When he was on a stretcher, he got hit in the knee.
Our 19 year old was evacuated back to the States.
He finished college and med school at a later date.
Maybe his thank you to that medic who sealed his fate.

12. Omaha Beach
"Before the Battle...plans are everything," Eisenhower said.
Paraphrasing, "After the first shot, you put the plans to bed."
At Omaha Beach nothing went according to plan.
The only constant was the thorough training of each man.
Officers and NCOs expected craters on the beach.
From small arms fire, they would be out of reach.
They expected fortifications and all the big guns
Would be blasted by the Navy and the bomber runs.
The way should be cleared by dozers and DD tanks.
Supporting artillery fire would decimate enemy ranks.
Nothing they expected happened that day.

The shoreline they trained for was somewhere far away.
The invaders were all seasick from hours at sea.
They were soaked and miserable as they could be.
Many who survived the landing had nothing to use.
They were let off in deep water by the landing craft crews.
Equipment was dropped to avoid being dragged down.
They came to fight the enemy, not to drown.
Naval artillery spotters had no radios on shore.
The demo men couldn't cut barbed wire. What's more
The obstacles weren't cleared for incoming boats.
They were skewered, and by mines they were smote.
Men who had arms stopped though things were dire.
Rifles needed disassembly and cleaning in order to fire.
The only cover was the beach by the sea wall.
Which protected them from some fire but not all.
Mortar rounds with their high arcs showered down.
It was only a matter of time. All were death bound.
The junior officers and noncoms with true grit
Knew what had to be done and did it.
Men who weren't infantry found weapons among the dead.
They went with the GIs and charged ahead.
The famous orders that mean the most in war.
"Follow me men." This is leadership to the core.
All were civilians barely two years before.

13. Pointe-Du-Hoc
This high cliff had a view of each American beach.
In both directions, Utah and Omaha were in reach.
Sited on top were several cannons of large bore.
They could blast landing craft or ships off the shore.
The Rangers were tasked with neutralizing this fort.
Naval gun fire blasted it but would come up short.
The battleship Texas used its 14 inch guns.
Destroyers took a turn coming close in their runs.
Reinforced concrete can withstand direct hits.

The only result was piles of rock broken to bits.
Some 200 well trained men in top shape made it to land.
As in other operations, nothing went as planned.
German machine guns hit with enfilading fire.
It seemed only luck prevented results most dire.
Some equipment was lost, but they went ahead.
Scaling the 130 foot cliffs was the cause of dread.
At London's fire department ladders had been found.
They were mounted on DUKWs but needed firm ground.
Only one could be raised, but it was a flop.
It waved all over the cliff face with one guy on top.
They fired rockets trailing rope up the side.
Being completely soaked, it was too heavy for the ride.
Finally, they got three lines up with grappling hooks.
Men were able to climb. Bravery and strength it took.
More lines were dropped. The whole party got there.
The German defenders died or fled from their lair.
Then disappointment when the Rangers reached their goal.
The German 155 cannons turned out to be telephone poles.
People have heard this, but read on my friends.
The rest of the story has a meaningful end.
They fought a German detachment in a fortified house nearby.
Then went on to pursue their next objective by and by.
Rangers found the guns that they had sought.
Some 250 yards inland, they had been brought.
Thermite bombs were used to destroy the guts of each gun,
Then they blew up an ammo dump while having their fun.
The Germans counterattacked. The Rangers held out.
Only 50 were able to fight at the end of the bout.
Other Rangers coming from Utah helped in the German's
    rout.

14. Brief Thoughts
Extreme
The most extreme experience a person could go through

Was being a Marine or Infantryman in World War II
In Europe the worst of the extremes was Omaha Beach.
Waiting for death or charging into the breach.

Father

Father L was too old to go ashore with the dangers,
But he went anyway. He was chaplain to the Rangers.
He gave a little pep talk before they hit the beach.
"Men, I don't want to see anybody praying within my reach.
If I do, I'll give you a boot in the rear.
Your job is to fight. Mine's to pray. Am I clear?"
Father L did more than pray on that day.
He pulled men from the surf and out of harm's way.

A Drink

He climbed the path and rested on the bluff.
Nobody was there. Did they all have enough?
There was just a dead German lying on the ground.
As he approached, he heard a whispered sound.
"Ein born." What did he mean? He pointed near.
There was a spring with water cold and clear.
He filled his canteen and took a long drought.
Then gave the German a drink. They so recently fought.
Killer to care giver in an instant. Who would have thought?

On Failure

Eisenhower said years later, if we had failed the D-Day attack.
"It would have been impossible to bring them back."
We had 2400 casualties on Omaha Beach that day.
While 34,000 landed to carry on the fray.

Bedford, Virginia

"The Big Red One," the 28th Division, part of the National
    Guard,
Going into Omaha Beach, they didn't expect it to be so hard.
Thirty Virginians in the 116th Infantry Regiment, Company
    A,
Were among the first to land on that bloody day.
They fought with courage, that's what Virginia men do.

Nineteen were dead before the day was through.
With a population of 3400, no town suffered more
Than Bedford, Virginia, in the Second World War.

15. The Hedgerows

With thousands planning the invasion on D-Day,
No one put thought about the next step along the way.
Aerial photos were taken, the hedgerows weren't in mind.
Apparently, they thought these were like the English kind.
Imagine horses jumping them while chasing a fox.
These would provide infantry cover maybe with a wall of
    rocks.
Then the reality presented itself to our advancing GIs.
The hedgerows were solid dirt, rocks, and roots six feet high.
Then brambles, vines, bushes, and trees reaching to the sky.
There was no easy way a soldier or even a tank to get by.
This type barrier surrounded each Normandy field,
Except for one gap for the cows, it was a perfect shield.
The fields and their hedgerows went on for miles.
These were perfect natural obstacles. Attack was futile.
Tanks couldn't push through but would mount up instead,
Presenting their soft bellies, one shell and they're dead.
A soldier could get through, he might have to hack away,
But he would be exposed to enemy fire that way.
Someone thought dynamite, but they'd need thousands of
    tons.
Then an inventive GI* found a way. This battle would be won.
The beach barricade steel was provided by the Krauts.
Pieces were welded to the tanks so they'd stick out.
Steel rails would penetrate the hedgerows and cut through.
The tanks would push forward, then blast the defending
    crews.
Phosphorous shells that burned hot were used in the main.
Thus, we were able to advance through the Normandy terrain
Our GIs were physically tough but also had brains.

*Sgt. Culin, formerly a cab driver, invented the Rhino tank.

16. The Sure Shot

Lieutenant W was a great bear of a man.
He weighed 250 pounds, kind of big for the airborne clan.
Some said he needed a bigger chute with his weight.
Others said he needed none with legs that great.
The lieutenant was an outdoorsman through and through.
It's said he never missed. One bullet would always do.
He went out on recon to scout the land,
And heard German spoken, though he didn't understand.
He yelled "Hande hoch" as he jumped into the field.
Seven officers didn't question and started to yield.
The eighth pulled his pistol and was shot on the spot.
Two others started firing from the other end of the lot.
The lieutenant got several holes in his clothes and lost half an
    ear.
He dropped to one knee and without showing any fear,
He shot the seven as they tried to run away.
Then dove into a ditch changing a clip where he lay.
He carefully killed the two Jerries at 100 yards.
Ten dead for ten shots, no shot was too hard.
He was just like Sergeant York in the First World War.
Every general wished he had thousands more.

17. Advice to a Replacement

After being in combat for a week or two,
We all learned survival. There are things you just do.
If you stop for a few minutes, dig a hole. Why?
This will save your life when shells land nearby.
Sometimes the Jerries have artillery observation posts.
They see you stop. That's when the shells come in the most.
You'll learn by the sound if they're coming your way,
And when to hit the ground and if you should stay.
You'd climb inside your helmet to soften the blow,

But it's only going to protect your head you know.
Fear is inevitable, it's something you'll find,
That's manageable and can be controlled by your mind.
We've been completely trained. We all decided it's true.
They can't teach you about combat. Learning is up to you.

18. Judging Men

Each company had a guy who bragged and talked tough.
Maybe he excelled in training, but he didn't have the right
  stuff.
He was first to break when things really got rough.
Then there's the quiet guy you hardly notice in camp.
He becomes heroic the minute they drop the ramp.
Nobody would ever guess he'd be the champ.

19. Spotters

We landed small plane parts on the beach on D-Day.
The Piper Cub had to be assembled before getting under way.
When airborne, they flew low and slow.
To spot targets, enemy emplacements below.
The Germans learned to fear them and ran away,
Since within a short time, naval shells came their way.
When we moved inland, we were beyond range of the naval
  guns.
We had no way to call in aircraft making attack runs.
We tried colored smoke and bright sheets on the ground.
Neither proved suitable, it was quickly found.
We got the idea of radios linking ground to air.
A GI spotter or a tank was closer to the Krauts' lair.
Also, when a tank was "buttoned up," the crew wasn't aware,
While the infantry couldn't tell them of targets out there.
The solution was a phone on the tank's back for talk.
An infantryman could spot targets as he walked.
These improvements became available at a quick pace.
Not only were we inventive, we were in an arms race.

20. St. Lo

When we fought through the hedgerows, the goal was St. Lo.
This small Normandy city was where we must go.
St. Lo was a road hub, to both sides it had import.
We needed it in our quest for Cherbourg, the port.
The fighting was hard though we developed techniques
To blast through each barrier for the goal we did seek.
From the beach to St. Lo it took 40 days.
Casualties were high as we battled away.
The 90th Division, for example, was really three it was found.
One in the field, one in the hospital, and one in the ground.
Casualties were 100% among the enlisted men.
It was about 150% among the junior officers then.
Bad for us, that July was the wettest in 40 years,
Keeping our air support down until the skies were clear.
However, the B-17s blasted St. Lo when it didn't rain,
Leaving nothing but rubble covering the terrain.
The local people suffered in the battle every day.
Their stone houses were forts to be overrun along the way.
Also, every church steeple was blasted from the sky,
German ob posts were there since they were high.
We got to Cherbourg ten days from then.
It was pretty much destroyed by the defending men.
It took six more weeks to get it functioning again.

Chapter 14. Breakout

1. Operation Cobra

For almost seven weeks we'd been ashore.

The fight through the hedgerows was a continuing chore.

We built 12 airstrips near the Normandy beach.

Response time was short. Our targets were easy to reach.

Two panzer divisions arrived traveling at night.

They were positioned opposite us ready to fight.

With our Jabos continuing to be on call,

The Germans couldn't easily attack at all.

The famous blitzkrieg was reduced to waiting and dug in.

They knew the big attack was soon to begin.

The Germans had nothing behind them with empty roads.

We had traffic jams, material arriving by the loads.

A plan was hatched. Cobra was its name.

We would blast the Krauts and send them back where they
    came.

It started off with P-47 rocket and bomb attacks,

Followed by 1800 B-17s, a fleet miles front to back.

Then the B-26s and P-47s had another go.

Thousands of artillery guns added to the show.

Over 16,000 tons of bombs and 50,000 shells

Created for the panzers a literal hell.

A lot of this was random, but we had spotters too.

Both Piper Cubs and troops radioed targets to gun crews.

Unfortunately, too many bombs and shells fell short,

And over 100 of our men were killed by this ground support.

Attack! To our divisions the order went out.

The panzers were hurt, but there was still fight in the Kraut.

It took two days, then the breakout came.

No defensive positions 'til the border, the Siegfried Line by
    name.

We activated the Third Army with Patton in charge.
With our Normandy breakout, the effect was large.

2. Retreat

The German command broke down. They fled in disarray.
Much of their equipment was left or thrown away.
Every man for himself. It was a rout.
Forget loyalty to squad or fatherland, just get out.
Patton wanted to keep pushing no matter what.
Cooler heads prevailed. Our supply lines could be cut.
The Third Army moved south and then east.
Hitler had a plan to tame the American beast.
He ordered six panzer divisions to attack west toward the sea.
This would sever Patton's supply lines as easy as can be.
Now we had an opportunity to cut off the Hun attack.
In retrospect it could have meant we'd both be set back.
Our new plan was for Patton to turn toward the north.
While for the Brits, south is where they should go forth.
We had to close what was called the Falaise gap,
A tricky procedure ripe for mishap.
We had one advantage. We held the hill at Mortain.
From here we had a view of the local terrain.
It turned out the Germans couldn't get their way.
The men on Mortain held out for five days.
The panzer divisions had no choice but retreat.
Many avoided our trap which we couldn't complete.*
Patton was incensed at the failure, mad as can be.
"I'd create another Dunkirk and drive the Hun and Brit into
    the sea.
We didn't get them all. They continued to flee.
*Monty couldn't or wouldn't drive south.

3. Hill 317, Mortain

Hitler commanded the panzers to drive west.
They attacked at night and surrounded Hill 317 in their quest.

The command of 2nd battalion, 120th regiment was captured
    then.
Leaving Captain E in control of some 700 men.
The 30th Division was in the path of the panzer attack.
It was an overwhelming force that pushed us back.

"For a better view I'm going to climb to that ridge line.
Sargent, take your radio. Under that overhang is fine."
"Careful, sir. Make sure they don't see the binocular's
    reflection.
Of all ways, that's the easiest means of detection."
"I figure seeing me and hitting me are two different things.
I'm guessing there's no sharpshooters. I won't get dinged."
Lieutenant W was part of an observation post.
Forward observers had more value than most.
They'd spot a target, find the coordinates on the map,
Then radio the information. In a moment there's a
    thunderclap.
Either artillery would blast or a diving plane,
The German target was destroyed, most everyone slain.
The Jerries had to eliminate this thorn in their side.
They couldn't move forward. They had nowhere to hide.
Six men or more were observing the Hun,
With enough targets around them for everyone.
The stationary German targets got artillery fire.
The aircraft* responded to moving targets they could acquire.
Some targets were found in daylight from the smoking gun.
At night muzzle flashes determined the location of the Hun.
Soon the men were out of food and medical stuff,
And small arms ammo was low. If that's not enough,
The radio batteries started failing. If they did, that's the end.
Resupply was tried with parachutes from their friends.
These blew away, so they shot artillery shells.
The stuff they contained was broken to hell.
Lieutenant W continued for five days with a rare rest,

When finally the panzers stopped their drive to the west.
With little sleep or food he called in 193 missions.
The panzers couldn't move forward because of his precision.
When it was over, he wrote a letter to his dad.
"Not much going on here," was what he said.
This may be the biggest understatement we had.
*P-47 Thunderbolts or British Typhoons.

4. Brief Notes

Tit for Tat

"Ach, here comes an ambulance. Lost I'd say.
Turn around. We won't shoot you. Go on your way."
A few hours later, the same ambulance appeared.
It stopped, and the driver got out. His meaning was clear.
"Was ist los." The German approached the military chest.
It was full of American cigarettes. Who would have guessed?

Tat for Tit

The Polish captain approached leading a group of men.
"Please take these prisoners and put them in your pen."
"No room, I can't help you. What's that paper say?
You don't have 1500. What happened on the way?"
"Oh, we shot them"."Why not shoot everyone?"
Quietly, "Truthfully, we ran out of ammo before we were
     done."
Maybe not excusable but payback time for the Pole.
His countrymen suffered the same fate, reversing their roles.

Normandy's End

We charged out of Normandy. On Aug 25th Paris was free.
The Germans didn't want to destroy it. Toward home they
     did flee.
The battle of Normandy was over. It lasted 75 days.
Our Allies and we had 200,000 casualties along the way.
This included 40,000 dead, 2/3 of them ours.
Considering we were on the attack, not too dour.
Of the 450,000 German defenders less than 10% got away.

A tremendous fraction surrendered to live another day.
Of 1500 tanks, those remaining that crossed the Seine, just
    24.
They left 3500 artillery guns and 20,000 vehicles more.
The escaping men had one thought, at home they'd fight their
    war.

5. The Invasion of Southern France*

"Anvil" was the name when this invasion was in planning.
It was to compliment "Sledgehammer", the northern landing.
"Overlord" was later chosen to designate D-Day,
While Anvil became "Dragoon". Churchill didn't have his
    way.
He felt he had been dragooned into going along.
He preferred the Balkans. Everyone else thought this wrong.
There were two reasons why this landing zone was best.
We wished to trap the Hun in France's south and west,
And two ports were available there.
Getting supplies ashore was a problem quite severe.
The Germans had depleted the divisions in that part of
    France.
They removed equipment. The unfit soldiers didn't stand
    much chance.
Only one panzer division was available for defense.
Their job was to slow down the Allies advance.
The other divisions consisted of non-Germans from the east.
Plus the physically challenged whose military duty should
    have ceased.**
The French resistance's contribution was a great addition.
They blew bridges and disrupted communications to help the
    mission.
Before the landing our Air Force bombed away.
A multi-national airborne unit landed early that day.
Their prime job was securing the high ground.
They also destroyed any coastal artillery they found.

Commando units landed on nearby island beaches
To help keep our men out of the Hun's artillery reach.
Our landing went well. Casualties were light.
Most beaches were secured with a minimal fight.
We landed 200,000 men and secured the ports.
The destruction of piers and docks were the Hun's last resort.
Our army moved north, the resistance lesser or greater.
We made contact with Patton's army 26 days later.
The outcome was as expected as the Germans fled.
We had 3000 killed, light but blood is always shed.
*Aug, 15, 1944
**Such as one legged veterans.

6. Young Audie Murphy

Born to a sharecropping family back in '25,
Audie was sixth of twelve kids. They scratched to stay alive.
That life was hard in the best of times.
During the Great Depression an hour's work earned a dime.
That is if you could find work of any kind.
When his father ran off, it put them in a real bind.
Audie left school after fifth grade to help support.
He did what he could in rural Texas, work of any sort.
He picked cotton, he plowed fields, he helped in a store.
Audie worked in a radio repair shop and maybe more.
He became an expert marksman hunting for small game.
A friend commented that he always hit at what he aimed.
His reply was, "If I miss, my family won't eat today.
Every time he went on a hunt, it was not play.
When he was 15, his mother up and died.
All could not be supported no matter how hard they tried.
They placed the three youngest in an orphanage to ensure
     their care.
At war's end Audie reclaimed them getting them out of there.
After Pearl Harbor at 16, he tried enlisting, not a whim.
The Marines, the paratroopers, and the Navy all rejected him.

Being less than 5 ½ feet tall with a baby face,
This slim young man wasn't wanted any place.
Finally, after doctoring his birth certificate a bit,
The Army took him though they felt he didn't fit.
His first commander wanted to send him to cooking school.
Audie finished basic training persistent as a mule.
People may picture a military hero in their mind.
I'm sure Audie Murphy is not what they would find.
But the military could always use more of his kind.

7. Audie in Combat

Audie finished infantry school and then shipped out.
In North Africa he saw no action in the Axis' rout.
He was in the Sicily invasion of August '43.
His marksmanship showed. He shot two officers trying to flee.
Audie was in the Salerno and Anzio campaigns on the Italian
    front.
In each battle he showed his value as a grunt.
After being in combat in Italy for almost a year,
Audie's unit invaded Southern France with no time in the
    rear.
His best friend was killed by a German with a trick.
The Kraut feigned surrender (what an enemy to pick).
Audie Murphy went on a rampage and wiped out that gun
    crew.
He destroyed several more positions before he was through.
For this he received the Distinguished Service Cross.
In every heroic action he reduced our GIs' loss.
Audie got field promotions and medals along the way.
He was second lieutenant and company commander on the
    fateful day.
In January of '45 his company had only 18 men left.
There were 128 to start with. Life is war's theft.
The Germans pushed forward. Murphy sent his men to the
    rear.

He stayed and picked off attackers never showing his fear.
He ran out of ammo, then mounted a tank destroyer on fire,
And used its machine gun. For the attackers the effect was
    dire.
After an hour and wounded, Audie got his troops to enter the
    fray.
They counterattacked the Germans and drove them away.
The Medal of Honor was awarded for his actions that day
Audie Murphy received 33 medals, everyone possible from
    the USA.
The French and Belgians added six more to say thanks.
Audie was the most decorated soldier in our ranks.
He had multiple wounds and earned three Purple Hearts.
He fought having malaria which he got at the start.
This 110 pound boy of 17 turned 20, and it's hard to
    comprehend.
He put on 35 pounds and 1 ½ inches by the war's end.
Audie wrote his memoirs after the war.
"To Hell and Back" was a best seller and more.
Audie stared in the movie for his encore.

8. Across France

The last month of the summer we charged across France.
To some the war was almost over at first glance.
We linked up with the Seventh Army coming from the south.
They had landed near Marseilles by the Rhone River mouth.
German troops were fleeing by foot, bike, and truck,
Which they'd commandeered and drove 'til they ran out of
    luck.
Vehicles were only good as long as there was gas.
When this ran out, they stopped on the roadside grass.
The Krauts had little ammo and no rations were left.
They foraged for food. You could call it theft.
As we charged along, we found a warning sign.
If there were people, gifts, and flowers, all was fine.

Otherwise, the Huns were still occupying that place.
We used care in our approach and slackened our pace.
Some units advanced up to 50km per day.
On occasion, they had to blast roadblocks along the way.
Then as we approached the German boarder,
We had outrun our supplies and faced disorder.
First there was little fuel for trucks or tanks.
Artillery ammo had to be rationed for Brits and Yanks.
Even so, some units penetrated the Hun's defensive line.
Then had to pull back and wait for a time.
We had supplies in Normandy piled on high.
We even had a gasoline pipeline providing a good supply.
But our attacking troops had to sit and wait.
The Germans had time to reorganize at a high rate.
In defending occupied France, they wouldn't make a stand.
They were willing and able to fight for the Fatherland

9. Steve the Trucker

Steve was hoping to serve in the Army Air Corps.
Instead they trained him to unload ships, a stevedore.
He figured what the heck, I'll eat hot food and have a cot.
Then two months after D-Day he found his slot.
The Army had little supply from any real port,
And of truck drivers, they surely were short.
The drivers were mostly African-Americans trained on the
    spot.
They learned by doing is as likely as not.
In July from Normandy, the Army had broken out.
The Germans were fleeing. It was almost a rout.
We were trying to supply ours advancing to the east.
It was happening so fast, like lightning greased.
We organized a truck supply system that couldn't fail,
Since our bombing had eliminated the French rail.
Each truck had a red ball painted on the side.
The troops who manned them drove with pride.

They named the operation the Red Ball Express
After the railroad term when speed was stressed.
Our 28 divisions needed rapid resupply
Of ammunition, fuel, food, all needed to get by.
It was a 700 mile round trip. They made it in a day
With an east road and a west road, each one way.
The red ball trucks had right-of-way by law.
They drove faster than any trucks you ever saw.
Those 6000 trucks carried more than 12,000 tons
Each day with their high speed runs.
Drivers took turns at the wheel. They slept on the go.
They ate cold meals and drank luke warm joe.
Fortunately, the driving lasted twelve weeks, not a lot.
The city of Antwerp was opened, a big harbor spot.
And then Steve got his hot meals and a cot.

Chapter 15. Europe, The Fall of 1944

1. Operation Market Garden

We were low on supplies, the Siegfried Line lay ahead.
Blasting through this barrier would leave many dead.
An alternate plan was to attack to the north.
In one operation through the Netherlands, we'd go forth.
We had to cross several rivers including the Rhine.
Bridges over these had to be safeguarded along the line.
The allied airborne corps included two divisions of ours.
They were ready for action radiating power.
Airborne would capture each bridge, both ends.
A British armored column from the south we would send.
This operation was tricky. Nothing could go wrong.
The whole thing would collapse if the defense was too strong.
The paratroops landed and overcame a lot.
With high casualties they conquered each spot,
Except for the final place, the bridge that was too far.
We didn't know a panzer division was there for R and R.
The airborne were lightly armed, nothing for fighting a tank.
With no possibility of defending themselves, our chances
    shrank.
Meanwhile the Brits' armored column moved up one road.
Surrounding fields were too soft and couldn't support a load.
Fire from the sides immobilized the column on its path.
Our forward speed was reduced from the defender's wrath.
We didn't get to the last bridge and had to withdraw.
We had planned an attack that violated military law.
Don't ever try an operation where everything has to go right.
There is always the unforeseen in every fight.
From this time the poor Dutch suffered yet again.
They were punished since they welcomed our men.
Starvation for the next eight months happened then.

2. Fort Driant

Patton's Third Army had advanced to the east,
Toward the southern realm of the Nazi beast.
They were blocked by an ancient fort updated for the current
war.
With all the obstacles on Normandy's coast, this had more.
Fort Driant was surrounded by a moat deep and wide.
There were no obvious openings to get inside.
In the old type castles, walls could be broken apart,
But after bombardment, the concrete was as strong as at the
start.
Guns could be raised and fired, then drop from sight.
Scattered pillboxes, barbed wire, tunnels worsened our
plight.
Germans could pop out and fire a round,
Then drop back into some hole in the ground.
Tunnels interlocked the entire fortress inside.
Heavy steel doors couldn't be blasted wide.
The worst of all was when the GIs gained the top.
Neighboring forts fired artillery without stop.
The men said, "Everything we've tried came up short.
We should retire and develop new techniques to conquer this
fort."
Officers, leaders of the attacking men, told Patton the score.
He replied, "Never, if it takes every soldier in the Twentieth
Corps."
Finally, after ten days, we broke off the attack,
The Third Army's first defeat, but they'd be back.

3. Antwerp

The up river city Antwerp was the biggest European port.
We had liberated it, but the effort came up short.
By Sept. 15 the Germans had fled the city.
At the time we didn't take advantage, what a pity.

Instead of clearing the Hun between Antwerp and the sea.
Our effort was on Market Garden, a big error you'll agree.
We needed that port open as our short supply line
For ammo and fuel to attack the Nazi swine.
After diddling around, Montgomery, commander in the north
Finally consented to drive the defending Germans forth.
The estuary was cleared by November twenty eight.
For any autumn campaign, this was rather late.
Then the weather turned bad, but that's fate.

4. The Schu Mine

Our GIs found a new bane at the Siegfried Line.
The Krauts had developed another devastating mine.
The Schu mine was simple and could be made very cheap,
The Germans made millions. They were hard to sweep.
It was a pottery container or a box of wood
Holding an explosive charge. It blew up where you stood.
With only a tiny metal detonator, they could only be found
By a brave GI probing with bayonet in the ground.
The Schu wasn't meant to kill or blow up a tank,
But to blow off a foot and thus thin our ranks.
The GIs discovered a tank could set off the Schu,
So they were safe where a tank track had moved through.

5. The Siegfried Line

How many slaves did the Nazis use in the war?
Not known, of the work battalions, they were the core.
Not only did they build coastal defense, the Atlantic Wall,
But the German border defense, our attack to stall.
From Switzerland to Holland stretched the Siegfried Line.
The first defensive section to cross were fields of mines.
The S-mine or Bouncing Betty was feared by our GIs.
A spring shot it in the air, what a surprise.
S-mines carried a load of steel balls or scrap.
Which would blow off a leg or emasculate a chap.

Behind the mines a concrete apron they poured,
Up to 100 feet wide and a yard thick or more.
Pyramid shaped dragon teeth were mounted on this
Of varying heights and randomly spaced so a tank couldn't
    miss.
Behind these were concrete pillboxes, observation posts
With machine guns. Artillery could be called in on attacking
    hosts.
Barbed wire and more mines were placed here as well,
Crossing this line meant attackers were entering hell.
So they could cross fire, the pillboxes were properly spaced.
These supported each other when the enemy was faced.
More pillboxes were placed in additional rows.
Foxholes and trenches helped to vanquish their foes.
Completing the scene were a network of good roads,
And artillery batteries to deliver shells by the load.
The most formidable defense ever contrived by man,
To breach the Siegfried Line required new techniques and
    plans.

6. Breaking Through*

Division 30 was the first to break through the line.
A variety of softening blows we had to refine.
First recon flights took thousands of photos from the air.
Only at Normandy could the coverage compare.
Detailed maps were prepared, every squad had one.
We knew where the pillboxes were as well as each gun.
Next, a six day artillery barrage blasted away.
This was not for the concrete but to prepare the way
By exploding mines, stripping camouflage, and cutting barbed
    wire.
Next came medium bombers, but their targets weren't
    acquired.
As in other places, the big bombers weren't so hot.
In supporting ground troops they couldn't hit the right spot.

Short range mortars then bombarded the Kraut
With some 10,000 shells against the redoubt.
Finally, tanks hit the pillboxes firing at a continuous rate.
This didn't destroy them but it sealed the Jerries' fate.
They couldn't return fire. GIs could get to their rear.
Our engineers blew off the steel doors with little fear.
If the Krauts were quick, they could surrender then.
Otherwise they were killed, a grenade in their den.
The ground attack took just four days to complete.
The German impenetrable fortress we'd learned to defeat.
Later we tried a new technique against the Hun.
A point blank shot destroyed a pillbox from a 155mm gun.
*This section of the line was the westernmost of two lines.

7. The Interview

"Tell me about this company, whatever comes to mind."
"Well, I had some preconceived ideas. It's not what I find.
I'm a captain. Makes me wonder how I got here.
No training can prepare you for this military career.
How can anyone send these boys into battle?
They're too young. Sometimes we treat them like cattle.
They'd die for each other. Hell, they'd die for me.
Let me tell you about these two wire men, heroes you'll agree.
Shells cut the phone line. They go to do the repair.
They'd just finished when another shell hit there.
They were both wounded. To the field hospital they're sent.
Then pretty soon they're back, AWOL they went.
They felt guilty being away from the action and their friends.
This determination and loyalty, it just never ends.
So I want to reward them, a pass to Paris for six days.
The next day one of the lieutenants pokes his head in and
        says,
"Those two wire men don't want to go. That's their plan."
"Go tell them okay. Get two others if you can.
Can I lead guys like this? Am I enough of a man?"

8. Deadly Autumn

Our advance had really slowed down to a crawl.
Patton's army went 400 miles in August. Then came the fall.
After our supplies caught up, the offense resumed.
The quick victory didn't happen as people assumed.
Over 3 ½ months Patton's troops only managed 25 miles.
This was a war of attrition, a stupid fighting style.
Farther north the Hurtgen Forest was chosen to attack.
The planners never realized how the Kraut could fight back.
The forest was unlike any they had ever seen
With trees every few feet, all evergreen.
No vehicle could move there, and even the GIs
Had to duck under branches just shoulder high.
We had no forward observers. You couldn't see but ten yards.
There was no way to detect the Huns' defensive guards.
The few roads became quagmires quite fast,
And mines were planted to give tanks a blast.
No high rank officers visited men at the front.
They never knew how the GIs were taking the brunt.
Attack! Move forward! Kill the no good Krauts.
The effect was some units were quickly knocked out.
The rains came with mud, then the bitter cold.
Trench foot and battle fatigue took both meek and bold.
The jerks in the rear made trench foot a court marshal offense.
As if men tried to freeze their feet. Some officers are dense.
As casualties increased, individual replacements arrived,
Often poorly trained or not at all, these quickly died.
New divisions came in and also faced the gore.
Here we spent the best of the classes of '43 and '44.
I would call the battle of Hurtgen a criminal act.
There was no real reason to fight in that forest tract.
A military law: don't waste men in fruitless attacks.
Only probe a new terrain 'til you find a crack.

Use your strength, not overwhelming manpower which you
   lack.

9. Repple Depple

This stands for replacement depot in GI speak.
Replacement (someone was wounded or killed) makes things
   bleak.
Think of the poor teenager who arrives by ship.
First comes a reception depot after his long trip.
This is the second place where he knows not a soul.
He's all alone in this world. What is his role?
He stays or goes when there's an order to proceed.
Next comes the "stockage" depot where he gets what he needs.
This may be the first place he's touched a gun.
Not everyone passing through has even seen one.
Draftees may be trained for some other specialty,
But here everyone gets assigned to the infantry.
A few days later comes the repple depple, where he's assigned.
These aren't reserve units, but those on the front line.
Being a replacement is like being far, far away.
From everyone you know, lost and lonesome every day.
You are driven, then you march up to the front.
No training or advice, and you soon take the brunt.
The veterans, those who were in combat a week or two
Didn't want to be friends with the guys who were new.
Maybe it was bad luck. They attracted enemy fire in many
   ways.
Half the replacements were casualties in three days.
A million men went through the RD system during war time.
Many felt those responsible should be charged with war
   crimes.
Each man should have been integrated into a unit before
   seeing action.
He'd stand a better chance, thus raising the survival fraction.

10. Foxholes

The value of a foxhole soon became apparent to each GI.
It protected you from small arms and shrapnel flying by.
Most wounds and death resulted from artillery fire.
In your foxhole only a direct hit would cause you to expire.
In the months of fighting on the German border on the west.
Foxholes became home, a refuge, a place you could rest.
Think of a hole, just right for a coffin to fit.
This was the size for two GIs* though it seems a pit.
With the Winter the ground was frozen hard as rock.
There was no way to dig through. It required a shock.
If dynamite was available, it could blast through the ice.
Otherwise, a hand grenade would have to suffice.
With time, improvements could be made, like a log roof.
A tent half (each GI had one) made it "waterproof."
A low spot would collect water that got in.
A layer of pine bows kept it from your skin.
It is unthinkable, but we faced the cold with no Winter gear.
It wasn't distributed since the war's end was near.
Finally, each GI got a blanket, sharing meant two.
Body heat helped some, what else could you do?
The GIs' boots were not waterproof at all.
You were supposed to dry them at night, what gall.
The only way was to keep boots next to your skin.
The same for your socks, in neither case could you win.
In most wars both sides hunker down in the cold.
Not in this war, nothing was put on hold.
*One GI was supposed to be awake at all times.

Chapter 16. Europe, The Bulge and the Winter, 1945

1. The Bulge

Hitler planned offensives with no military training.

Early in the war, plans worked with hardly any straining.

The opposition was unprepared, and you could call them weak.

Surprise attacks resulted in quite a winning streak.

In late '44 the Germans were back within their borders.

A westerly offensive to squash the Allies was their order.

After the Allies guaranteed defeat, they would sue for peace.

Then Germany would beat the Russians advancing in the east.

Drive through the Ardennes Forest and push them to the sea.

Separate the Allies. Pound them and watch them flee.

Cut the supply lines of the British so they'll evacuate.

They won't expect our attack on a winter date.

Only four tired divisions guarded this segment of the west

They were stationed there for recuperation and much needed rest.

With 20 divisions including seven armored, the Nazis attacked in force.

They'd get to Bastogne and kill the Yanks with no remorse.

Why Bastogne? For the area it was a vital hub.

Quickly gaining this road center would be the rub.

The Allies expected quiet. Completely unaware they were.

The German buildup went unnoticed. It caused no stir.

Early on December 16, the artillery barrage began.

The first step of the German offensive plan.

They had plenty of troops, guns, and their fabled tanks.

Was this enough to dislodge those tired defending Yanks?

2. Stand Fast

"Sarge, I hear rumbling. It's an artillery attack."
"Go wake the lieutenant. Get him out of the sack."
"No, Dear, it's too early. I need my sleep."
"But, sir, something's happening. We may be in deep."
The platoon was a forward observation post.
It had been quiet here, German probes at most.
The lieutenant got out of his bag, a sorry sight.
The men took turns staying awake at night.
"I hear engine noise. Listen between each shell."
This could be a panzer attack, for infantry a hell.
"Call the command post. Tell them what we know.
Maybe the Germans will be putting on a show."
"Everybody up, take a leak, and eat a bit.
Rifles loaded and ready, no lights to be lit.
Shoes on and tied, grenades out and ready.
We have orders, only fire on command, be steady.
Sarge, take six men over to positions on the right.
Oh crap, I see four tanks, infantry are in sight.
Pick a target, aim as best you can.
Make every shot count, now fire, every man."
Many Germans dropped, both wounded and dead.
Winooski fired his bazooka, and one tank lost its tread.
Tank turrets turned. Last shots the GIs did fire.
They dropped into their foxholes, the bottoms filled with
     mire.
Two tanks hit the mark, two shots were high.
Half the men were casualties. Of these most would die.
Thank God, American shells began to hit.
Three tanks turned around and high tailed it.
The order came down. Hold positions at all cost.
Many did their duty, and many lives were lost.

3. The Battle*

They were hungry. They shivered in the cold.

Sometimes they retreated, but mostly they'd hold.
They hugged the mud when bombs and shells fell.
These troops thought they had entered hell.
They cursed the enemy and then their own side.
Mostly they held their ground where they died.
Some mastered their fear, some were mastered by it.
Some had the luck while some had not a whit.
Most of them fought hard and with skill.
Others held back for a lack of will.
Bullets and shrapnel didn't distinguish between,
Nor did death in that Winter battle scene.
*Adapted from a passage in "Bastogne, the Road Back,"
By Peter Elstob, Ballantine Books, 1968.

4. SS (Schutzstaffel)

The SS panzer divisions contained elite type troops.
They were rough and tough. I'd call them stupes.
About 150 Americans were prisoners of war.
The SS did what all would abhor.
They marched the men to a field and opened fire.
An act like this is guaranteed to raise ire.
Eighty men were killed. The rest took flight.
Then the order came down that very night.
All SS were to be shot on sight.
You see why their act was not too bright.

5. Be Wise

A wise philosophy when winning a war,
Treat POWs well, and you may get more.
"Fight to the death" has less allure.
A hot meal and a cot are better for sure.

6. Nuts

The Germans were advancing. The outcome looked grim.
The defensive perimeter shrank 'til it was pretty slim.

Each platoon and squad held their positions as told.
Men faught heroically 'til their blood ran cold.
Surrender or retreat only when ammunition ran out.
Then fall back. It wasn't a rout.
Each engagement held up the German advance.
Each hour delay was a victory for our persistence.
The weather was too bad for aircraft to fly.
The men needed everything that they could supply.
Our fighter bombers would certainly help out.
Those P-38 Lightnings had quite a clout.
Our leadership called the 101st up to the front.
They took up positions, the German attack to blunt.
Bastogne became their bastion to defend.
Here if necessary they'd fight to the very end.
The German Army surrounded the city cutting the road,
And stopping our truck fleet, the normal supply mode.
Then suddenly the sky's thick clouds cleared.
The C-47 Dakotas flew in. Our troops cheered.
Parachutes delivered ammunition, medical supplies, and food.
Dropping from the sky they brightened everyone's mood.
Lightnings attacked anything that moved, especially tanks.
For the fly boys more than one GI gave thanks.
When the fighting was heavy, the Germans sent an envoy.
The offer was to surrender or be destroyed.
General Mcauliffe, the commander of the one-o-one
Gave a one word answer. It was not in fun.
The word which has gone down in history is "nuts".
When you're surrounded by a superior force, this takes guts.
In retrospect we know the Germans could not win.
They didn't have enough fuel, and they were spread too thin.
They couldn't supply their troops. We had control of the air.
Plus two nearby armies were mobile and got there.
To avoid a pincer the Germans had to retreat.
After three weeks their great offensive had been beat.
They lost 1900 aircraft and innumerable tanks.

Over 200,000 killed and captured thinned their ranks.
For our victory there, uncounted heros get our thanks,

7. January 1945
Valley Forge comes to mind thinking of Winter war.
The troops' suffering has entered history's lore.
They did have shelter with tents and some huts.
Fire provided warmth and hot food, though not a glut.
They were not engaged in continuous fights,
And could lie on crude bunks to pass the night.
Contrast this with conditions in northwest Europe in '45.
Our men faced cold so brutal, they were lucky to survive.
The coldest Winter that section of Europe ever had.
At least in recent times, it had never been so bad.
Our men finally got sleeping bags and clothes for snow,
Though trench foot continued to lay men low.
The fighting didn't stop after the Bulge was done.
In fact the Germans invaded again. They weren't on the run.
The "North Wind" attack was aimed at France.
Hitler hoped to give his men at the Bulge a better chance.
He wished to stop the reinforcements there.
The new attack wasn't prepared with enough care.
The French Maginot line was finally used in defense.
We found it worked quite well, its effect immense.
This was one of the few times we could use a fort in the war.
We destroyed the attacking Huns 'til they wanted no more.
We slugged it out and by January's end
Had regained the land lost with a message to send.
Hitler, we are coming, unconditional surrender we intend.

8. February 1945
The Siegfried Line was the next objective to fall.
Resistance was mixed along this defensive wall.
Some sections had nobody home on the line,
So our attackers only had to watch out for mines.

At other places the Huns were tenacious in their defense.
We had to use our entire bombardment sequence.
Some Germans surrendered the first chance they got.
Others fought on and on until they were shot.
In the north we moved east and crossed the river Roer.
This had dams we had to protect for later in the war.
If they let go, the lower Rhine would be harder to cross.
Its flooding would be the Nazis' gain and our loss.
All along the front we advanced onto a plain.
This is the hardest type to defend of all terrains.
Hitler gave the order. No retreat. Fight to the end.
Never give up ground. Germany you should defend.
With our overwhelming air power, 11,000 sorties a day,
And our thousands of artillery pieces pounding away,
The Huns fell back 'til they could retreat no more.
Bridges over the Rhine had been blown by the score.
With no ammo and no possibility of resupply,
Some 250,000 of the Wehrmacht surrendered rather than die.
Two big cities suffered from our attacking force.
Aachen and Cologne became rubble in the war's course.
It was the German's choice, no need to fight door to door.
In both cities only the cathedrals remained at the core.
Devine protection, or we saw no need to punish them more.

9. Stay Awake

"I'm sitting here and feeling kind of strange.
My turn to stay alert. It's quiet for a change.
I'll keep my mind busy. I'll think about back there.
My folks, my brother and sisters, my love Clair.
I love them all. Now love's a funny word.
We love God. Loving all our fellow men is absurd.
Each kind of love's different, for my sisters and brother,
Different for our father, different for our mother.
I'm sure the deepest love is between husband and wife.
Maybe we love our squad most. For them we'd give our life.

But that's only for now, because of all this strife.
Loving my neighbor like myself is what I should do,
Which means I better make sure I love myself too.
Even if I don't love my enemy, I should act right.
Then I can still love myself long after this fight.

10. A GI's Prayer

Dear Lord, as we go into battle this day,
There are a few things that I want to say.
First, an apology for things I've done wrong in my life.
None of them were really so bad in this world of strife.
Mostly, they were sins of omission. I guess like most kids
I didn't say thank you, or I'm sorry for things I did.
I want to ask some favors for all my friends.
Please help them survive until the war's end.
Could we end this catastrophe before Joey comes of age.
I don't want my little brother to experience this outrage.
Please help my family grieve, and go on, if I die.
They know I love them all. We'll meet by and by.
And for me, please help me to be brave and a man.
I'll try to help my buddies however I can.
Here we go, Lord. If I say wish me luck,
I don't mean to be sacrilegious. I promise to duck.
I don't want to know the how or the when.
Just help me if it's part of your plan, Amen.

Chapter 17. Crossing the Rhine to the End, 1945

1. Remagen*

We were approaching the Rhine at a fast rate.
Piper Cubs flitted about, the enemy to locate.
One spotter saw the structure rising through fog and smoke.
By God it was a railroad bridge, and it wasn't broken.
Germans were retreating across. They'd laid out planks.
Quickly the news was passed up the ranks.
Secure that bridge. Establish a toehold on the other side.
Lieutenant T of company A got the order they did decide.
Some men said, "No way. They'll blow it. It's not okay."
Lt. T just replied, "Get going," and led the way.
Carefully running without stepping in a hole,
They dodged left and right seeking their goal.
Up ahead was an explosion. The bridge rose a bit,
Then settled back. It wasn't damaged a whit.
Engineers followed the infantry armed with snips.
They cut every wire at a quick clip.
Thirty pound bundles of TNT were cut free,
And dropped into the Rhine. Brave men you'll agree.
Infantrymen took care of snipers including those above.
Germans occupied the towers and required a shove.
They surrendered, and we chucked all guns we could find.
They're probably still resting on the bottom of the Rhine.
The squad that first reached the eastern shore
Had five ethnic groups who wanted to settle the score.
Sgt. D, a Czech-American was in the fore.
The tunnel at the bridge's end was secured with speed.
Most Huns were in no mood to fight, you see.
Take the high ground, had been drummed in,
Which they accomplished with their desire to win.

*Mar. 7, 1945

2. Engineers
We've read about engineers doing demolition and clearing
     mines.
They really outdid themselves when we got to the Rhine.
After we crossed the bridge, artillery pounded each side.
We had Piper Cub spotters. On the Hun we spied.
We targeted their buildup. They targeted our men.
A German shell hit the bridge now and then.
The Krauts even fired V-2s and attacked from the air.
There were plans to send frogmen. They gave us a scare.
The engineers made repairs and put booms upstream
To keep explosives from floating in with a demo team.
Meanwhile we labored to put a pontoon bridge across.
Strong currents had to be conquered with minimal loss.
We utilized Higgins boats to hold sections in place
Until the thousand foot bridge occupied its space.
A heavy cable was run the full length,
To anchor each pontoon and give it strength.
Completed in just 27 hours, though we worked with care,
In the first seven days 2500 vehicles crossed there.
The railroad bridge stood for ten days in all,
Then crashed taking 28 men with its fall.
By that time we had six pontoon bridges astride,
And had delivered nine divisions to the other side.

3. Patton Crosses the Rhine*
Two weeks after the first crossing of the Rhine,
Patton's Third Army got through at Oppenheim.
There was no bridge, and the Huns were unaware.
We crossed by boat to make a toehold there.
Starting at night we got our first units ashore.
Soon a pontoon bridge was assembled, then more.
By dawn we had more than a division across.

All was accomplished with little loss.
The Germans infiltrated military students with English skills.
By dawn they were all captured or killed.
The Hun made feeble attempts with air attacks.
Artillery fired, but neither could hold us back.
In less than a day we had three divisions on the east bank.
These were fully equipped including trucks and tanks.
All this was accomplished with no advanced prep.
No airborne, no smoke screen, no heavy bombardment step.
We gave up waiting for Monty's army in the north.
He had to have everything just right to go forth.
With two crossings already made, he wouldn't be first.
"Why didn't we go along with the plan," he cursed?
Meanwhile Patton did what he'd planned for a long time.
He walked to the middle of the bridge and peed into the
    Rhine.
*May 22, 1945

4. Monty's Ninth Army Crosses the Rhine*

Most of the Ninth Army were Canadian and Brits.
Though we had a major part to play in it.
Over 2000 of our artillery fired 65,000 shells or more,
Which we kept up until assault boats reached the shore.
Then we targeted spots that were farther away,
Huns and their equipment that would enter the fray.
The assault boats were small craft carrying seven men.
They dropped each load, then again and again.
Over 1400 of our B-17s pounded the drop zones and nearby
    land.
The Brit 6th and our 17th Airborne were part of the air attack
    band.
Some 3000 fighters provided cover and escort all around,
As well as support for the troops advancing on the ground.
A great fleet of transports pulled gliders and carried airborne.
We even had B-24s drop supplies on that morn.

Some 9500 planes were in the air over the Rhine.
It took some three hours for this fleet to pass that line.
The strangest part of this military operation,
Reporters and dignitaries were present, like a celebration.
Both Churchill and Eisenhower wanted to watch the show.
The start of the final act, delivering the blow.
*Mar. 23, 1945

5. The Flying Jeep
Gliders were towed by C-47s, two per plane.
This was the first time doubling. Pilots thought it was insane.
They were slow enough, an easy target from below.
C-47s weren't speedy, but this was just too slow.
Over 1300 gliders were towed across the Rhine
Airborne, supplies, equipment, if it was light then fine.
The gliders were just canvas covering a frame of wood.
Protection from bullets and shells was just no good.
Almost every glider had to make a crash landing.
Controls were shot up, so they were difficult handling.
One carried a Jeep. Start your engine they said.
An explosion cut the restraints. The driver thought he was
      dead.
The glider's nose broke free. Pilots and Jeep did too.
Would anyone survive this, driver or air crew?
The Jeep made a perfect landing on all four wheels
All three men survived uninjured from their ordeal.
The glider crews were not trained to fight with guns,
But they formed up as a unit when their flying job was done.

6. Surrendering
After the Rhine crossing, we advanced with speed.
We surrounded the industrial Ruhr. The Hun army was in
      need.
Most Wehrmacht surrendered, It was sensible to do.
Why die for a lost cause? Germany was all through.

A funny sidelight concerned a B-24 that crashed.
The crew survived and were taken prisoner rather fast.
The Germans kept them guarded while they checked around.
One spoke good English and told them what they found.
"You're winning it seems. We want to surrender to you.
Please take us prisoner. With this war we are through."
This is the only time a bomber crew took prisoners of war.
If there'd been a larger group, they could have taken more.
One procedure really irked our advancing men.
Some Huns fought 'til they ran out of ammo, and then
They'd put out the white flag, "We'll surrender now."
Why try to kill us first, if that's your plan anyhow?
There were still fanatics in the Krauts' defense.
The SS, Hitler youth, super patriots had feelings most intense.
They were determined to fight to the very last.
Postponing the inevitable though the die was cast.
In one German village some surrendered with white sheets.
The SS took all such people and hung them in the streets.
Meanwhile thousands walked west not even under guard.
Our only interaction was directing them to a POW yard.
Often an American teenager, dirty, hungry, and tired
Watched over a thousand Huns often more properly attired.
Some German officers, shaved, starched, and neat
Insisted on surrendering to a high rank in their defeat.
No grimy 20 year old looie, his requirements would meet.

7. Playing at War

Hitler in his insanity as he approached his end,
Thought of ways to carry on, no matter the trend.
He sent out the Hitler Youth, brainwashed for years.
Boys who should have been in school with their peers.
They carried the latest weapons of war.
Like the very effective panzerfaust and more.
The boys would lie in wait, and fire at a tank.
Then run into the woods like they'd pulled a prank.

They slowed our attack and upset the GIs.
After getting this far, they didn't want to die.
If the kids hid in a village and than attacked,
They'd get the full treatment when we fired back.
Then the 15 year olds who thought of the glory,
Found what real war was like, deadly and gory.
More than one young survivor was found cringing in fear,
Calling for mom when he thought death was near.
A kindly GI gave him a candy bar and sent him to the rear.

8. The Camp

The end of the European war was at hand.
The GIs knew it as they charged across the land.
They approached a camp. Nothing seemed to fit.
What is this place? There's barbed wire around it.
Be careful of a trap. Approach with care.
The men opened the door and could only stare.
The barracks were filled with people dying.
Starvation is a terrible sight. Some GIs were crying.
The captain came up and wished that he had not.
"For God's sake, don't feed them. It will kill them on the
    spot."
They brought up a field kitchen to make thin soups,
But kindness killed many. More agony for our troops.
High ranking officers arrived with frowns on each face.
The men had fanned out to search the place.
Then rifle fire from out back was heard.
The GIs had practiced some frontier justice it appeared.
They had rounded up every guard they could find.
Maybe someday this would provide them peace of mind.
The officers argued about what they should do.
Court marshal or quietly bury the dead and hope no one else
    knew.
This secret remained untold for many years.

No investigation ever happened. For the guards there were no
 tears.
Maybe some must talk as their own death nears.
I just know justice was dealt, though without cheers.

9. Finders Keepers
When the Nazi armies advanced early in the war,
They looted museums. In retreat they took more.
Jewish victims, when they were taken away,
Had all their property and business' stolen that day.
The wealthy had their homes stripped of all art.
Of this, the Nazi big shots took a large part.
What art objects the German government could find,
Was to be stored at Merkers in a deep salt mine.
In addition, the trove held a hundred tons of gold.
Most came from Nazi victims' teeth, pretty cold.
Our men had advanced and saw the hoard.
Trains were waiting*, some plunder still onboard.
We took all the art to Frankfort to store.
The museum pieces were restored after the war.
The gold was taken by our government to keep.
Was more gold sunk in Alpine lakes quite deep?
It's thought some Nazi bigwigs fled with big wealth.
There's no doubt Swiss bankers got more through stealth.
Of course, the true owners are dead and gone.
How do you distribute wealth gotten from such a wrong?
*Ironically, due to the Easter holiday.

10. American POWs
As we moved into Germany, we worried about our POWs'
 fate.
Could we save some 90,000, or would we be too late?
Many stalags (prison camps) were spread all over the land.
The POWs' condition was unknown. Could they walk or even
 stand?

We made one rescue mission plan. It seemed like a stunt.
It would require a 25 mile incursion beyond the front.
General Patton's son-in-law was a prisoner there.
A bit too much nepotism, but the General really cared.
The raiding party managed to get in all right.
The guards ran away with no desire to fight.
Then we found 2500 men, ten times the expected amount.
None were in good shape, a big problem to surmount.
They were given a choice, only a few could ride.
The rest would walk or remain back inside.
Most chose to remain "safe" in their yard.
They'd wait for our advancing army. Walking was too hard.
Unfortunately, the rescue team had to fight to get out.
There was still too much resistance left in the Kraut.
Many GIs were killed. Former prisoners were taken back.
They had to wait a bit longer for a successful attack.
Then typically, a few GIs would arrive at a prison gate,
And have to blow it open for the POWs to vacate.
Men rushed out shouting and cheering. Was this real?
Free at last. Many just wept due to their ordeal.
Then the rescuers endured hugs and handshakes,
Kisses and back slaps, almost more than they could take.
Many POWs were down to 100 pounds.
Lack of food and medical care had ground them down.
Surprisingly, less than one percent of Americans had died.
None had been slave laborers for the other side.
We did well. Russian POW treatment could be called
    homicide.

11. Those Nice People
As our armies advanced to Germany's inner parts,
The GIs found things that gave them a start.
Civilians seemed in general to be rather nice.
Maybe conquered people do what will suffice
To placate the invaders and not make them mad.

They had suffered enough with their homegrown cads.
Many GIs made comments about what was seen.
The towns and villages were always quite clean.
Even war's rubble often was quickly removed.
The people's hard work ethic was so proved.
The Germans went to church, and seemed to follow the rules.
Why were we fighting? Were we all a bunch of fools?
They were just like us, until we entered hell.
We came to areas with this overwhelming smell.
Human bodies were being burned in a large pile.
Concentration camps were found with conditions most vile.
Hitler's final solution of the Jewish problem was here.
Starve them, gas them, or work them under conditions severe.
All these nice civilians said they didn't know.
Many were brought there. They had to be shown.
Our Fuhrer would never have ordered this.
His underlings must be those most remiss.
The truth is the German people really knew.
Intelligent, hard working, religious, none of this came
    through.
If we had our own Fuhrer, would we act the same too?

12. Berlin

The hell with stopping, charge ahead to Berlin.
This was the call, seeing the trouble Germany was in.
Eisenhower knew what the Yalta conference decided.
After the war was done, Germany was to be divided.
If we continued east, we'd be in the Russian zone.
We'd have to give up land that we had won.
We approached the Elbe River and stopped there.
Two allied armies converging have to take care.
It was decided earlier what Berlin would cost.
An estimate of 100,000 casualties, too many lives lost.
Better that the Russians pay this price.
They didn't care. They never treated their soldiers nice.

Besides, two operations had to be done.
We had decoded Russian messages concerning land to be
    won.
They wanted Denmark, so they could control the Baltic Sea.
The Brits in the north diverted to keep the Danes free.
Also, in the south we knew of a Nazi plan.
Hitler wanted the Germans to fight to the last man.
Code named "Werewolf", they would fortify the mounts.
These are easy to defend where every man counts.
We had no desire to fight the Hun on this terrain.
Our southern armies diverted, this plan to contain.
By this time few Germans were paying attention to him.
Werewolf was just propaganda, a crazy dictator's whim.
East meet west at the Elbe River line.
GIs and their counterparts met and all was fine.
For a short while we could sing, drink, and dine.

13. Points

"Attention. At ease.
Okay men, we're all aware the war's coming to an end.
We got a directive about letters you may send.
Don't presume you'll be going home soon.
Don't tell your loved ones about any potential boon.
We're going to have to form an army of occupation.
Plus, the Japanese have to be defeated by our nation.
As I read it, all of us will get a point rating.
After what we've been through, it's rather frustrating.
We'll get points for time in combat and overseas.
Extra for wounds received and the right type disease.
That doesn't include anything you get from a lady friend.
So don't try any shenanigans if that's what you intend.
You fathers out there get a special break.
The Army gives you points for the kids' sake.
Receiving medals gets the most. After getting the tote,
The GIs with the most get to climb on a boat.

This may seem unfair, especially if we go to Japan.
We did our part already. Now each has to be a man.
The Army needs you, so buck up. I know you can.
That's it. Dismissed."

14. Survivors

Three years and five months after Pearl Harbor to the day.
The war in Europe ended on the seventh of May.
Eleven months plus one day from the Normandy beach,
Fighting for yards or miles 'til victory was in reach.
Most infantry units had a complete turnover then.
Some had almost three times that with replacement men.
Did anyone from the first three divisions ashore,
Make it to the surrender being continuously at war?
Did anyone wind up unwounded during that fight?
If so, he was the luckiest man in my sight.
It was certainly bad for the enlisted GIs.
For the junior officers it was worse, no surprise.
When you lead men, you lead from the front.
The Krauts' fire was directed, and you took the brunt.
Most survivors in the infantry are proud they were there.
They proved to themselves they could do their share.
The invasion of Europe was a great adventure for them,
But absolutely none would want to do it again.

Chapter 18.   Medics and Corpsmen*

1. Medics
"Medic," the call goes out from the wounded or his buddy.
Some poor guy's got it. His body's all bloody.
The medic's job is first aid. Try to keep him alive.
Stop the bleeding, clear his airway, try to revive.
He works on th GI, but he's exposed to fire.
He can't do his job while lying in the mire.
He has to squat or kneel. He's not flat on the ground.
Knowing full well there'll be a sniper who'll give him a round.
He will sew or bandage, give a shot of morphine, try to do no harm.
Start a bottle of plasma, or splint a broken arm.
Then place him on a stretcher. Carry him to the rear.
They'll get a Jeep with litter racks. From the battle field they'll clear.
Then to the field hospital or MASH he'll be hauled.
It's <u>M</u>obile <u>A</u>rmy <u>S</u>urgical <u>H</u>ospital**, but it wasn't so called.
The picture I'll always have in my mind I've found,
Is that of a rifle with bayonet stuck in the ground.
This is holding a plasma bottle, the liquid of life
Keeping some poor GI going amidst war's strife.
It's said that 85% reached by a medic and still alive
With good treatment at the MASH, survived.
Most medics were conscientious objectors in the war.
People against violence but among the bravest by far.
*The Navy and Marine equivalent
**Adopted after the war

2. Penicillin
In this history there's a story that must be told.
How the wounded GIs' lives were saved by mold.

This was the first time in all of America's wars,
Less died from disease. Wounds and accidents caused more.
First in '35 sulfa drugs were invented, but didn't have the pep.
These couldn't touch pneumococci, staph, and strep.
The story of penicillin starts back in '28.
It was discovered by Alex Fleming, but we had to wait.
He found it in mold, and it could kill bad germs.
Not many people were interested and no drug firms.
One clinician tried it on a very sick man.
His condition improved but not according to plan.
There was not enough penicillin, and the patient died.
It was too hard to obtain, no matter what they tried.
Most studies were done in Britain before the war.
In '41 we got interested. We knew what was in store.
There was an available lab in Peoria, Illinois.
They hoped corn could be used. That was their ploy.
First they needed a better strain of mold.
One Mary Hart found it on cantaloupes. This was the gold.
With war effort speed, many plants started work.
As in all our industries, no one shirked.
We produced enough to treat 100,000 in '43.
This reached four million in '45, a production spree.
No one knows how many allied troops were spared.
Penicillin did its job. The death rate was pared.
Penicillin is one of the greatest inventions ever made.
All the antibiotics sprang forth in a medical parade.
Its importance in medicine will never fade.

3. The Doctor

The wounded keep coming. Will it ever end?
We sort them out. That's the modern trend.
Those who can wait, those who can't, those who'll die
No matter what we do, no matter how hard we try.
I can't stand this life, but it's what I chose to do.
I must keep going 'til this war is all through.

As a doctor I must detach myself from the gore.
That's the only way to maintain my sanity in this war.
They're just boys and even those who are not,
Never pictured themselves blown up or shot.
I read the dog tags. Maybe it's better not to know
The name of some poor kid who'll never be able to grow.
Maybe if I just talk to the ones who survive.
They've gotten that chance. Will they stay alive?
Here's one who lost his lower leg, poor guy.
"Hi, Doc. I survived. I'm not going to die."
"No, Son. Life is going to be tough, but you'll get by.
It will be a battle. Now's the time to really try."
"I know, Sir. My Dad says, 'I am the master of my fate.'"
"That's the spirit. By God, that's really great.
I'm going to take your Dad's advice. It's what I've sought."
And so by the patient the physician is taught.

4. Wounded

GI: "What's that up there. The light's so bright.
People nearby are all dressed in white.
Dear Lord, I have some questions for you.
Am I in Heaven, cause I haven't a clue?
I didn't think I'd ever make it. I'm not good enough.
Sometimes I wasn't kind. I tried to be too tough.
Why do the Angels cover each mouth and nose?
Do they wear glasses? That I'd never suppose.
Gee, now I feel some pain and my gut aches.
I thought that didn't happen for goodness sakes."
MD: "He's coming around. Welcome back, soldier. It was
    close.
The nurses will take over and give you a dose."
GI: "I don't know what's going on. Is he God?"
RN: "No, though he thinks he is. When the pain stops give a
    nod.
This isn't Heaven, well maybe compared to the front line."

GI: "It's Heaven to me. You can be my special angel, all mine.
Do I have to go back? I hate that life.
I'll stay here with you. Will you be my wife?"
Is it a million dollar wound for this GI?
Maybe it means Stateside when time goes by.
Maybe the proposal will be accepted, the lucky guy.

5. The Million Dollar Wound

When veterans talked, it was quite clear.
Every GI thought this. They didn't want to be here.
Each thought he was invincible before combat's start.
After seeing enough wounded and dead there's a change of
    heart.
Then they thought luck had been with them so far.
Would that luck hold out to the end of the war?
Don't screw up. Keep everything the same if you can.
Do your best to stay clear of fate's bad plan.
Then they figured the next bullet had their name on it.
Their luck had run out. They'd soon be hit.
There was thought of a wound somewhere along the line.
Not the minor kind which would be a bad sign.
They'd patch you up and send you back to the front.
But not a serious wound either where you take luck's brunt.
Just the right type wound to get you out of here.
It's a 'million dollar wound" and will make you cheer.
You may be hurt, but you'll recover within a year.

6. Medic Tales

We are used to the movies where the wounded want to die.
There's no reason to live without an arm or after losing an eye.
No medic ever heard this. If they did, they wouldn't comply.
More likely they'd hear a wounded GI say,
"Take care of my buddy. He's hurt bad. I'm okay."
His last words in this lifetime. Then he passed away.

7. Doctor Interview

"Doctor, about the medics, could you make a comment or
    two?"

"Sure, I've got a hell of a lot of respect for everything they do.

They got a lot of noise in training in the States,

Stuff about cowardice and not having what it takes.

It's about not wanting to kill and refusing to carry a gun.

That became completely reversed when we faced the Hun.

Now they get total respect, justifiably so.

When a guy's wounded, then they really know.

It's flat out heroic being exposed while treating a man.

Knowing some Jerries will hit you if they can.

These men are in their twenties, at least most are,

Not as young as a lot of the GIs but on a par.

They were trained in special courses at college.

It required the ability to study to gain the knowledge.

It's all about first aid, so the wounded don't die.

They have to think fast, do treatment on the fly.

Last week one did a tracheotomy with seconds to spare.

He opened the kid's airway and placed a tube from his pen
    there.

Saved his life and as neat as a surgeon could do.

Hell, I've seen safety pins and sewing thread too.

They run out of sutures, so they use what they've got.

No wasted effort, act now, get it done on the dot.

I've told several, they're for me if I'm really in need.

If my life's in the balance, I like their speed.

Maybe if they make it, they'll go to med school.

They could do emergency work, always keeping their cool.

Now if you'll excuse me, I've got wounded back there.

I'm saving up my break time for when no one needs care."

"Thank you, doctor. I know you do more than your share."

Chapter 19. The Pacific, 1945

1. The Battle of Iwo Jima*
Iwo is a small isle halfway between Saipan and Japan.
It was felt it would fit well in our strategic plan.
Three air strips filled the flat center of the isle.
These could provide for our aerial warfare style,
An emergency landing place for B-29s returning from raids,
Or a launching place for fighters acting as protective aids.
We would eliminate a Jap early warning site,
And any interceptors that they might send up to fight.
Later it was suggested Iwo would help to guarantee
The safety of bombers making the A-bomb delivery.
Maybe none of this would really count if we knew
How costly Iwo's conquest would be for our invading crew.
Some 22,000 defenders fought mostly 'til they died.
From 11 miles of tunnels the Japs had to be pried.
Tunnels connected pillboxes, bunkers, and hidden guns.
This was a new type of fighting. The Marines were stunned.
No one realized volcanic ash** was not like sand.
You couldn't dig a fox hole in this type land.
Our Marines did as they had to do though not as planned.
*Feb. 19-Mar. 26, 1945.
**The movie, "Sands of Iwo Jima" was misnamed.

2. Mount Suribachi
The Marines came ashore. There was no enemy fire.
Maybe with three days bombardment, they all had expired.
The Japs had a new doctrine. Be patient and wait.
When the Marines move inland, they'll meet their fate.
We got to the first row of bunkers. Then it began.
The beach was crowded. More waves had reached land.
Crossfire from Jap machine guns cut our men down.

Artillery blasted the beach with no cover to be found.
The Japs had fortified Suribachi, a steep mount.
They could fire down, and every shot would count.
One group of grunts fought across the isle.
This way the Japs couldn't reinforce the great rock pile.
The first day 30,000 Marines came ashore.
After the mount was taken, there'd be 40,000 more.
With determination and continuous bombardment there,
On the fifth day our men moved up with great care.
Patrols were the first to reach the top.
At least for the moment, the fierce resistance had stopped.
Others followed. One was bearing Old Glory.
They found a rusty pipe. Thus began a story.
The commander said, "I want a bigger flag there."
A photographer went along, an action shot to snare.
Yes, it was posed, but it was the most memorable photo of
    World War II.
Five Marines and a Naval corpsman were the flag raising crew.
Three of them were killed before the battle was through.
When the Marine Memorial was built near D.C.,
It was a replica of this photo that made history.

3. Iwo Jima Battle Concluded

With the mountain's capture conditions didn't seem so bright.
The north of the island was more prepared for a fight.
More bunkers and pillboxes dotted the land,
All connected with tunnels, so they could be remanned.
The Leathernecks could take a fort thinking all the Japs died.
Then later they'd attack from the rear when we passed by.
The Japs could even pull back with our approach,
And none would be killed when the barrier was broached.
We decided grenades and flame throwers worked the best.
Those mounted on tanks were better than the rest.
These were called "Ronsons" or "Zippos*" by the men.
They had a longer range for hitting the Jap dens.

Often the Japs attacked when it was quite dark.
Our ships launched star shells from where they were parked.
The Japs knew we bombarded before an attack.
We decided to forgo this and went when the night was black.
We'd catch the Japs asleep and unaware,
One of our easier wins, catching them in their lair.
Some Japs knew English and called for a corpsman's aid,
Whom they shot when his approach was made.
After a month the Japs were finally defeated.
It had cost us almost 7000 dead in battles most heated.
Of wounded, almost 20,000 were recorded.
Heroism was common with 27 Medals of Honor awarded.
Being an island, there was nowhere for the Japs to retreat.
Death or surrender were the choices when they were beat.
Only 216 were captured in the Japs' defeat.
*Cigarette lighters.

4. The Youngest Medal of Honor Recipient

"Grenades, grenades. Dive and cover your head."
That's about the only way not to wind up dead.
Jack knew the drill but dove the other way.
He landed on the grenades. Was this his final day?
Jack wanted to save his buddies, his only concern.
This came naturally, not a reaction you could ever learn.
Our hero got the Medal of Honor for his act.
He should have gotten another for surviving the attack.
He had more than 250 shrapnel pieces taken out.
Every organ got its share. His survival was in doubt.
Just 17, he was the youngest since the Civil War
Receiving this award. There is no higher score.
Jack forged his mother's signature when 14 years old.
The Marines took him, no questions asked, nothing told.
At 15 his age was found. They wanted to sent him home.
He said he'd go for the Army, so please leave him alone.
They had him driving trucks in Hawaii, a safe spot.

He snuck aboard a troop ship headed to where it was hot.
They let him join a fighting unit headed for the shore
Of Iwo Jima. One of the biggest battles of the Pacific war.
Afterward Jack went to business school and got a BS.
Then in the 60s joined the paratroopers where he was doubly
  blest.
He was bored and said he was afraid of heights.
Thus, his decision, a good one in his sight.
In a training jump, both parachutes failed to deploy.
Jack survived the fall. He was hard to destroy.
In both cases it was not Jack's time to die.
He lived to 80, and it took cancer to get this guy.
His last words were to his wife, "I ain't dead yet."
He had the last word. So died this outstanding Vet.

5. Bombing Japan*

The first use of the B-29 was from India bases.
These raids were targeted at Southeast Asia places.
We built runways in China for attacks against Japan.
Over six months, 12 raids were all we could plan.
Only one of these you could call big with 90 planes,
Getting supplies to these bases was a real pain.
All the fuel and bombs had to be flown from far away.
Bases needed Chinese protection to keep the Japs at bay.
All in all, this was too big a cost for little gain.
When the Mariana Islands became available, the decision was
  plain.
We had built two bases each on Tinian and Guam, and one on
  Saipan.
Altogether, 900 planes could fly toward Japan.
The Superfort was designed for high altitude and daylight.
Though many raids were flown low and at night.
Primarily, we hit cities with fire bomb attacks.
Japanese industry was spread out often in wood shacks.
Sometimes fire bombs burned whole sections of cities.

Japs desired to die for the Emperor, so we showed no pity.
One type mission of which most are unaware,
Was to interdict shipping. The B-29s did their share.
They dropped antiship mines in ports and sea lanes,
Helping our subs stop the Jap's supply chain.
The Japs used suicidal fighter planes to ram B-29s.
A pilot for an 11 man crew, for them was fine.
*First mission, June 1944.

6. The Okinawa Invasion*

We needed a base that was close to Japan,
Big enough to support its invasion was the plan.
Okinawa was located just right for us.
Being within fighter plane range was the big plus.
This was the last and largest invasion of the Pacific war.
More ships and planes were involved than anywhere before.
We landed 183,000 men, four Army divisions, two Marines.
The supporting armada was second only to the Normandy
    scene.
Okinawa and Iwo Jima were home islands, part of Japan.
Here we'd expect tenacious defense from every last man.
The Jap defenders included about 120,000 army and navy
    troops,
Supplemented by thousands of untrained local groups.
They even drafted teenage boys from an island middle school.
To expect young children to bear arms is rather cruel.
In one engagement they had women just armed with wooden
    spears.
When you charge against firearms, a deadly result is clear.
The local people and the Japs just didn't get along.
Okinawans were second class citizens, a continuing wrong.
Near the end of the campaign, some Japs tried to hide.
The local people would turn them in to our side.
The Okinawan language wasn't known by most Japs,
Making it easier to round them up with no mishaps.

*Apr. 1 to June 21 1945, 82 days, about as long as the
  liberation of France.

7. Okinawa Naval Battles

Our large fleet was there to protect the landing force.
Ships and planes bombarded the Japs, of course.
Transports stood by and landing craft shuttled toward land.
It was like Normandy, cargo being moved across the sand.
Unlike Europe, the Japs attacked mostly by air.
They unleashed their suicide Kamikaze* planes there.
Their goal was to crash into a ship and explode.
Sink enough ships and our attack would be slowed.
Kamikaze means "Devine Wind", the storm that saved Japan.
In ancient times attacking hoards' ships were destroyed before
  reaching land.
The Japs used several types of single engine planes.
Also, bombers could drop gliders with limited range.
Each carried a regular aerial bomb load.
It was a one way trip. No one returned in this mode.
More than 1900 attacks against our ships were made.
Our casualties exceeded any other naval battle in these raids.
We lost 12 destroyers and 15 amphibious boats this way.
While 368 ships and boats were damaged to our dismay.
Besides the air attacks, land based motor boats had a turn.
These were easier to intercept, blast, and burn.
I've often wondered how the Kamikaze got through.
Maybe pilot and plane were shredded while the bomb flew
  true.
The Japs sent in the "Yamoto", their strongest battleship, we'd
  never defeat.
It, plus 15 escorts were to sail directly into our fleet.
They would blast away, then beach themselves and fire at our
  landing force.
We intercepted this armada and sank it in due course.
The plan was for our men to approach only from one side.

It took 300 planes attacking for two hours before it died.
The technique worked, and the Yamoto blew apart and sank.
Only ten of our aircraft were lost. Dear Lord, thanks.
*First used in the Battle of Leyte Gulf.

8. The Okinawa Land Battle

Before the big landing, we invaded nearby isles.
Denying them to the enemy was worth our while.
We mounted artillery to bombard the defending Japs.
Land based guns were more accurate filling in Naval gaps.
The troops then landed on Okinawa's west side.
Resistance was light. The Japs had better places to hide.
We swept across the island. It was narrow but long.
Our GIs thought this would be easy. They were so wrong.
One force drove north. This campaign took three weeks.
The south was a much harder victory to seek.
Defense in depth was how the Japs made us pay.
They'd vacate their positions when we blasted away.,
Then quickly reoccupy and fight 'til we drove them out.
Some would fall back to the next position. It was never a rout.
As with every other island, they surrendered or died.
Since the former was never an option, many chose suicide.
Some 4000 sailors performed Seppuku, the ancient rite,
Where you'd cut open your belly. We'd rather die in a fight.
One of our Marines, a Hawaiian of Japanese descent,
Convinced many to surrender. He said what he meant.
Our policy was to treat our enemies with compassion.
Though GIs didn't always act in this fashion.
We lost some 12,000 killed in the Okinawa fight.
World War II casualties in April '45 hit their height.
The highest ranking general lost in the war,
Was Lieutenant General Buchner, Simon Bolivar.
On Okinawa we learned how the invasion of Japan would be.
We'd have to fight for every inch toward final victory.
The Japs would never give up. They'd fight to the death.

Everyone, including civilians, would resist to their last breath.
The taking of the main islands of Japan,
Would mean millions of casualties. We needed another plan.

9. Dave the Naval Officer

Dave had gone to college for a couple of years.
About the draft board he had some fears.
He knew they would send him where the need was most.
Better to volunteer. The Navy seemed the best post.
They said due to his college, he'd go to officer school.
Normally, in peacetime graduates fill the leadership pool.
After commissioning Dave served on a transport ship.
These were used in our invasion landing trips.
The ship was a relatively safe place to be.
Dave thanked God that he was out to sea.
Not a risky activity like the seamen faced
As they ferried soldiers or Marines to the landing place.
Dave's ship was in on the two Italian landings.
When they got to Normandy, their record was outstanding.
They had suffered no damage nor lost any men.
Soon they sailed back to the States when
They got word that after maintenance, they'd go to the Pacific.
Everyone knew they'd be fighting Japan to be specific.
No one knew their destination when they left port.
Even the captain found out only from a radio report.
Their convoy was headed in a northwesterly course.
They would be with the Okinawa landing force.
Little did Dave know of what was in store.
Their cargo of troops got safely to shore.
They remained on station to provide resupply,
When they experienced the hell that came from the sky.
The destroyers and escorts had formed a ring
To protect the fleet from Japan's latest thing.
Suicide bombers, the Kamikaze by name,
Dived out of the mist, toward his ship they came.

The ring of fire had not stopped one plane.
It crashed and exploded. This attack was insane.
The ship was ablaze. The sailors manned the hoses.
Finally, the fires were stopped. They counted noses.
Twenty dead, as many wounded. Dave was okay.
He had seen his friends just blown away.
These sights he cannot erase. They're with him to this day.
Japan was ready to surrender, some have said.
Tell this to the victims who wound up dead.
The Kamikaze attacks say they'd fight on instead.

10. The Indianapolis

She was a sleek ship commissioned in '32,
But she was a warrior through and through.
The Indianapolis earned ten battle stars in the Pacific.
She shot down planes and sank ships. She was terrific.
She was with the carrier task force that passed the test.
They helped stop the Jap conquest in the southwest.
After convoy duty she traveled north to the Aleutian Isles,
Where she bombarded Jap installations over many miles.
When the Aleutians were secured in '43,
She became the flagship for Admiral Spruance in the South
    Seas.
Now her primary job was to blast the enemy's shore
To prepare for the Marine's island hopping war.
She participated in the battles many will know,
Tarawa, Palue, Saipan, her eight inch guns delivered her blow.
Kwajalien, Tinian, Iwo Jima, Guam and Yap,
She even helped bombard the homeland of the Jap.
I would call her a lucky ship if I may.
She never received serious injury along the way.
That is until the Battle of Okinawa in '45,
Where an attack was made she was lucky to survive.
A Jap plane dropped its bomb before crashing at sea.
It passed through all decks. It exploded when breaking free.

The Indy was seriously wounded. She sailed home for repair.
She was under her own power the whole way there.
It took three months plus, limping home and in fixing the
    ship,
But as luck would have it, she was assigned an important trip.
Not knowing, the Indy delivered the atomic bomb parts
To the airbase on Tinian Island in the Pacific's heart.
It wasn't known, but we were near the end of the war.
Could anything happen? The Indy didn't know what was in
    store.

11. The Shark Attack
The Island of Guam was the Indianapolis' next stop.
Several sailors (lucky guys) there were dropped.
The Island of Leyte in the Philippines was next.
Who would know that the Indy was hexed?
There was no thought of subs, so no evasive action.
The captain figured Japan's waters would be their attraction.
Then on July 30 at 14 minutes past midnight they struck.
Two torpedoes ended the Indy's string of good luck.
She sank in 12 minutes. 300 died there.
No time to sent an SOS. No time to take care.
There were not enough rafts or even life vests.
The men dropped into the black sea with hope they'd be blest.
The Indy didn't make Leyte at the planned time and date.
No one seemed to take note that she was late
Three and a half days later on a routine patrol flight
Some survivors were spotted in the bright daylight.
The pilot radioed for help and dropped a radio and raft.
Aircraft and ships were directed there on the sailors' behalf.
A PBY directed a ship they flew over, the Doyle.
Time was important for death to foil.
Against all orders the PBY landed on the open sea,
And started picking up the survivors as quick as can be.
They loaded the plane until they ran out of room.

Then they tied sailors to the wings bending them, so the plane
was doomed.
The Doyle arrived in the night as black as pitch.
They stopped at the PBY and unloaded with no hitch.
Risking their own safety, they directed a searchlight at the sky.
This was a beacon for other rescuers to be guided by.
Of 1200 men that manned the Indy, 316 survived.
Many died in the water when the sharks arrived.
Some were dead from drowning or thirst.
Drinking salt water was a death that was worse.
The total dead from the Indy's sinking was the worst of the
war.
More died from shark attack than ever in history before.
And a final note on the fate of the PBY.
It was damaged too much, on the bottom it lies.

12. The Best Kept Secret
Nuclear physicists knew there was some way
That Einstein's theory could be brought into play.
Mass could be converted to energy. It was done in the sun.
Maybe a super weapon would help the war to be won.
European scientists had escaped to the west.
They knew Nazi Germany was making this quest.*
If Germany was successful, then all would be lost.
We had to beat them at any cost.
To President Roosevelt, Einstein sent a note with a plea,
Urging an all out effort by the land of the free.
A chain reaction was sustained by Fermi's team in '42.
The promise of a fission bomb seemed to be true.
The Manhattan Project was launched to develop the device.
Hundreds of thousands worked on it, no worry of the price.
Two installations required power in vast amounts,
Oak Ridge, Tennessee and Hanford, Washington were right
on all counts.
Los Alamos, New Mexico provided the directing lab.

Only the most important scientists knew what they had.
The secret was kept until the atom bomb's use.
All those workers kept quiet. No lips were loose.
To make sure the atom bomb worked as planned,
A test firing was tried on our own land.
At White Sands in Alamagordo, mounted on a tower,
"The Gadget" was detonated with unimaginable power.
Those watching exclaimed with total awe.
"What have we created?" A glimpse of hell is what they saw.
*It turned out, they couldn't succeed on the path they took.

13. The Delivery

In July of '45 the Japs were approached about ending the war.
Unconditional surrender was our demand, no less, no more.
The Jap government had a list of what they'd accept.
No occupation, no punishment, Korea and Formosa would be
    kept.
Given that Japan would never surrender to our will,
President Truman made the decision, so less blood would be
    spilled.
We had plans to invade Japan on November first.
It was estimated, with a million casualties we'd be cursed.
With the Japs' desire to die for the emperor in this fight,
Millions of men, women, and children would expire outright.
All things considered, the use of the bomb was just.
We would carry through as we knew we must.
Two B-29s had been altered so the bombs would fit.
They would take off from Tinian, Japan to hit.
Several targets were selected with careful thought.
Mid-sized cities over which we hadn't already fought.
The first plane, the "Enola* Gay" carried "Little Boy" by
    name.
A bomb built of uranium from which its power came.
Two other planes flew ahead, the weather to check.
With clear skies we could see all the way to the deck.

Were the weather bad, another city would do,
But Hiroshima got it. On August 6 the bomb blew.
No one had ever seen destruction so vast.
Most died instantly. For others the agony would last.
Three days later the "Bockscar" carried "Fat Man."
The city of Nagasaki was its target as planned.
From the manmade element plutonium, the second bomb was
   made.
This showed the world, in two ways we made the grade.
*Reversed it spells "alone" which the commander certainly
   was

14. POWs in Japan

Our biggest POW groups came from the Philippines, Guam,
   and Wake.
When you retreat, there are prisoners to take.
In our invasion of small isles, there was no getting away.
Any POWs the Japs had, they soon would slay.
The sinking of ships and the downing of planes
Provided POWs toward which the Japs weren't humane.
Those not beheaded, beaten or shot, every man
Was gathered together and shipped mostly to Japan.
POWs were used for slave labor working 16 hours a day.
They lived in filth. A starvation diet wasted them away.
Sadistic beatings were delivered for breaking a rule or not.
Medical treatment was non-existent. Sickness was their lot.
To maintain their sanity, the men developed techniques.
They communicated by morse code when forbidden to speak.
They stole bits of paper for writing notes and making plans.
Escape was always on their minds even from remote Japan.
Working outside the camp, they would sabotage what they
   could.
Some sand in a bearing might freeze a machine for good.
Moving material by backpack allowed them to steal.
Foodstuff was concealed in pant legs for a forbidden meal.

Even with their inventiveness many couldn't survive.
Some 37% of our POWs in Japan didn't leave alive.
Meanwhile only 1% died in the European theater of war.
The Nazis were bastards, but the Japs were so much more.
We fared better than the Chinese slaves there.
Of thousands only 50 survived the nightmare.
The Jap philosophy was they were worthless so who cares.

15. POW Letter

I know our letters will never be sent.
They gave us the chance, and we know where they went.
One of the guys saw them being burned out back.
These Japs are the cruelest, of humanity they lack.
So in my mind, I write to my dearest love Sue.
I tell her things so she won't worry, wouldn't you.
I describe the camp and all the great things we get,
And how my friends are doing, all the guys I've met..
I describe the swell food (my share of a stolen melon.
It was six seeds plus some pulp. Thank God for that felon.)
The medical care is great (the Japs packed my wound with
      dirt.
Maybe there's something to it, since it no longer hurts.)
I'm well clothed (they didn't steal my stuff.
I've worn my shirt for two years. It's durable enough.)
We're treated with compassion (Beetle Brow was going to beat
      the whole camp.
He stopped halfway through. We think he got a cramp.)
I thank her for the letters (none has ever come through.)
The Red Cross packages are welcome (they're two years
      overdue).
I'm glad to get the news of family and friends.
I imagine what's happening at the world's other end.
Dear Lord, my thoughts are a gift to keep me sane.
Please, with all this degradation, can I have a clear brain?
Someday it will all be but a memory long past.

Could you make it the short term type that doesn't last.

16. No More Prison Camp

The end of the war was approaching everyone knew.
POWs had seen the fleets of B-29s flying through.
Guards were acting differently. What was in store?
Would they all be executed? Japs could do more.
Threats of death had kept them in line.
An escape try meant ten would die. It was the fine.
The same could be expected for hitting a guard.
Punishment for any infraction was exceedingly hard.
Then one day through the camps a rumor spread.
An entire city was wiped out with everyone dead.
A week later a radio message could be heard,
Unconditional surrender was accepted, the emperor's word.
POWs still weren't sure what would happen next.
Their guards walked away leaving the men perplexed.
B-29s started to appear all flying low.
Their bomb bay doors were open. Watch out below.
Out tumbled pallets containing food of every kind.
Starving men gorged themselves. No one dined.
For some the dysentery continued unabated.
Their eating binge didn't stop. They weren't sated.
Then a wondrous thing happened. Those starving GIs
Gave food to the villagers who couldn't believe their eyes.
All the Japs had treated the POWs with disdain.
They were less than human to be tortured or slain.
Over 1500 B-29s dropped food to POWs all over Japan.
They knew the Japs would just as well starve every man.
The POWs still had to wait to be transported out.
What's a few days, they could all shout.
"We're going home. This nightmare is done."
But the memories continued for most everyone.
You don't forget such experiences though the war was won.

17. The End at Last

Think of all the men in the Pacific theater of war.
Think of those who fought in Europe, tired to the core.
Think of the young ones just entering the country's service,
Never having been in combat. All these were nervous.
They all could imagine what would happen next.
More years of combat, lives that were hexed.
The first bomb was delivered, then the second one.
The troops all knew what it meant, we'd won.
I can imagine the cheering. Give your buddy a hug.
Even those stiff generals would get out and cut a rug.*
Break out the beer. Maybe some saki was found.
Time to let it all go. Soon we'd be homeward bound.
Ask any GI, "What do you want the most?"
"I just want to go home. Get me to that west coast."
Some have said, the Japs were ready to quit.
The atom bombs weren't necessary, too big a hit.
After the Okinawa campaign, the GIs knew that wasn't true.
The Japs would fight to the end. It's what they do.
"That's it. We'll surrender," the emperor said.
Fortunately, most Japs obeyed, enough countrymen were
    dead.
On Sept. 2 the formal papers were all signed.
Japan surrendered unconditionally, not so bad they'd find.
The battleship Missouri played host on that date.
A gift to President Truman who hailed from that state.
*Dance.

Chapter 20. Afterward

1. Why, Ike?

Ike said, "God, I hate the Germans." There's more.
In the first years he hated them for their aggressive war,
For the misery they brought to countries they overran,
The senseless killing determined by Hitler's plan.
In '45 after the liberation of most of their empire,
He hated them for forcing him to destroy with bombs and fire.
He hated them for making him order young men into battle,
For conquering their army and herding them like cattle.
He hated them for fighting for an evil and hopeless cause.
Which was contrary to the Germans' best interest and laws.
Finally, he hated them for not calling a halt.
The complete destruction of their country was their own fault.

2. The Mother of Normandy

The paratroopers dropped form the sky.
They landed in the town square where they died.
Simone, a mother, watched the horror with her kids three.
The Americans had come to help set France free.
She took it upon herself in the following weeks
To care for their graves. No help did she seek.
Over 15,000 Americans were buried near there.
A picture appeared in Life magazine of her loving care.
She was decorating General Teddy Roosevelt Junior's grave.
He charged ashore on Utah beach. He was known to be brave.
Letters started arriving from parents in the States.
Could she take care of their son's grave? It would be great.
Could she send a picture to remember him by?
She took it upon herself to always reply.
Simone continued her noble task for 44 years.
She only stopped when her own death neared.

Thousands of American parents remember with their tears.
For Simone Recaud of Ste. Mere-Eglise our cheers.

3. Going Home
Boy I'm glad to be on board this old tub of a ship.
The Queen Mary would have gone at a faster clip.
With the war over we don't have to worry as we cross.
Better than the other way. Subs caused such loss.
I can stand the discomfort. I'll soon be home.
With this big wide world, I have no desire to roam.
Just give me my family's love and home cooked meals.
Both will do a lot to help my wounds heal.
I told Mom and Dad and my love Mary Lou
That I was wounded but not about all I went through.
I never mentioned that I lost one of my feet.
Will Mary Lou still love me since I'm no longer complete?
We used to dance just about every Saturday night.
They'll fix me up, though it may never be right.
I'm getting used to the crutches to help get around.
Doctor Jim said I'd do okay. Can't keep a good man down.
I won't be able to work in Dad's business as planned.
I'll have to find a desk job where I don't have to stand.
The lieutenant said I should get a college education.
He talked about government help from a grateful nation.
I'll have to look into that, talk to teachers back at school.
They've been to college and know I'm not a fool.
I don't know what I should take for a course,
Engineering or accounting. I'm sure teaching they'd endorse.
I'll get my leg fixed up first. Will I be peg leg?
Whatever, I'll be strong. For pity I'll never beg.
I've got time to think, and I shall persevere.
By God I'll prepare myself for a good career.
And if Mary Lou won't have me, I'll find another to hold dear.
One positive aspect of war, I learned to conquer my fear.

4. Charlie

Charlie was drafted at 29. He didn't want to fight.
He knew he had to serve since the cause was right.
Being a medic is what he volunteered to do.
He had to go to several schools. All he learned was new.
Charlie didn't mind since school was better than war.
He finally got to Europe in the Spring of '44.
At that time the Italian operation was getting slow.
The Allies were drawing off units for a different show.
The forgotten campaign was the invasion of the south of
    France.
Up the Rhone River Valley was their rapid advance.
Charlie was there helping wounded in the field.
German resistance stiffened. They no longer would yield.
Our medic was caught in the open with no escape.
He became a prisoner of war, a pretty bad scrape.
This was better than many medics got.
They worked without guards and often were purposefully
    shot.
The transportation to Germany was by railroad cattle car.
His POW experience left more than one scar.
Food for the men was in pretty short supply.
Mostly they had cabbage and fake bread quite dry.
That bread was ersatz, diluted with saw dust.
Our POWs were treated better than others, but just.
Charlie, the quiet man, was trusted by all.
For the job of dividing the bread, he got the call.
He survived his ordeal and was liberated at the end,
But like other men, he needed some time to mend.
Charlie never married. He was reclusive in his way.
Would his life have been different? None of us can say.
But war took its toll for the rest of his days.

5. Walt

Walt was in a bomber crew in the war.

Not a pilot or other officer. He'd say no more.
Years later he was married with two sons.
But the dreams kept coming about bombs and guns.
One night they were especially vivid to him.
He jumped out of bed and yelled with vim.
"The plane's on fire. Get out, get out."
Then he dove through the window with a shout.
Fortunately, Walt's family lived in a one floor house.
He was found on the lawn by his worried spouse.
A decision was made that very night.
They'll always live where there's a lack of height.
There are so many courses on memory skills.
Why not the opposite, maybe forgetting pills.

6. Robby, the Sniper

I was a sniper. We don't get taken prisoner, it's said.
Except when you're wounded, and no one's aware, or they
    think you're dead.
I know my buddies wouldn't have left me there.
My position was too remote. No one else was near.
My unit fell back. I couldn't follow with the pain.
I was taken prisoner. Wounded is better than being slain.
My luck held. The German who took me in was kind.
He could have just killed me on the spot, if of mind.
Other POWs and I wound up in Poland in the east.
Of all our problems, "where" seemed the very least.
We suffered privation with hardly anything to eat.
We were housed in wooden barracks with no heat.
There was no medicine. My leg wound wouldn't heal.
What's more important, a cure or a decent hot meal.
The Russians were coming. We were marched west.
My boots were gone. This put me to the test.
We marched for a hundred miles or more.
Walking in snow without shoes will make you sore.
Finally, we were liberated by the advancing GIs.

Maybe some medical attention would be my prize.
The doctor said we can't treat that wounded leg.
We'll have to amputate. "Oh no," I begged.
I refused treatment though the infection was bad.
My leg was still useful even with the workout it had.
Finally, I was released. The Army was through with me.
I took an old treatment that required the sea.
Run into the ocean. Stay there 'til you can stand no more.
Warm up for a few seconds, then repeat by the score.
And by God it was cured. My leg has been fine ever since.
I've worked hard my whole life with never a wince.
I'm here after 65 years thanks to my sea water rinse.

7. In Memoriam

I've gone to many services on Memorial Day.
They stir the emotions in more than one way.
Mostly, there's this tremendous sadness I feel,
And it's mixed with American patriotic zeal.
There is the anger. It is so wrong.
Why can't the world's people learn to get along.
In my sadness there's a point I wish to make.
Could people change something for the fallen's sake.
"They gave their lives," please don't say.
Their lives were taken, certainly not given away.

8. Loyalty

Men may join the service due to patriotic zeal.
"Rally around the flag boys," is how they feel.
Maybe it's to fight for country or king.
Perhaps it's loyalty to emperor, that's their thing.
But it all changes when the bullets fly.
These reasons mentioned are not why they die.
They die for their buddies. It's what they do.
There is a bond there for every member of the crew.
Nowhere else in human endeavor is this true.

9. Let Us Forget

We should remember that all war is hell.
This should be burned on our brain and hearts as well.
But for the soldiers who've experienced it, forgetting is best,
The details that eat at your guts and the rest.
"I want to remember that innocent young guy.
I wanted to protect him, like a brother is why.
He shouldn't be there, not in that hellish war.
He should have been back home just doing his chores.
But I wish I could forget the way that he died,
Blown apart like that while at my side."
"I know what we did was necessary to do.
Those damn Japs would not surrender, it's true.
But I have this picture, in my mind it's framed.
One running from the cave engulfed in flame.
He screamed, I know from unbearable pain.
Then he writhed for a bit 'til death made its claim."
"Dear Lord, there's one memory I want no more.
We liberated this concentration camp late in the war.
All those prisoners, they were just bone and skin.
To starve people like that is the worst kind of sin.
I shouldn't have looked, but then I must.
We had to help them, in God we all had to trust."
Dear Lord, help these poor souls. Relieve their pain.
Good men shouldn't suffer. Could you alter each brain.
We all have selective memories, it's true.
Why not selective forgetfulness too?

10. Survivor Guilt

Why do survivors often suffer some guilt?
Maybe it's just the way good men are built.
Our minds may wonder why we're the lucky ones.
Only a few survived when the battle was done.
"My buddy and I got out of the prison camp alive.
After a few years back home, we thrived.

Why wasn't I among the dead?
Why did my life turn out so great instead?"
Thankfulness should reign, but guilt takes its place.
Bad dreams and thoughts fill the mental space.
Meanwhile those psychopaths who cause all the pain,
Sleep like babies and are guilt free in the main,
A strange mental quirk that none can explain.

11. Modern Patriots

Born in the twenties, prosperity but not for all.
Teenagers in the Great Depression, the economy in free fall.
Servicemen in the forties, they faced maiming and death.
After the war, they worked and studied without a breath.
In the fifties, they bought the house, they raised the kids.
They worked so they'd have it easier than Dad did.
Send them to college, maybe their lives will be great.
But what's this? All the GIs stood for, their kids hate.
From love of country and all it stands for.
In one generation, of patriotism they want no more.
They could still love their country though they hate a war.
Freedom means working to change what you abhor.
Their Dad risked it all. They burned his flag.
This symbol of our country they treat like a rag.
Shame on them. Treat the flag with unfailing respect.
The Greatest Generation suffered, the flag to protect.

12. Could We Do It Again?

World War II was the biggest event in the history of men.
Could something like it ever happen again?
There's a very good reason why the answer is no.
An aggressive nation could start with a conventional blow,
But if one combatant realized it would lose the war,
The nuclear weapons would come out to even the score.
No one could build up a force for a D-Day attack.
Satellites would detect this. The other side would fight back.

What about our country, could we do as we had done.
To stop some expansionist country? China could be the one.
Unfortunately, our elite have frittered our manufacturing away.
We still can produce trucks and aircraft to this day.
But our ship building is essentially gone. We produce too little
steel.
We can make some stuff, but not enough I feel.
We import too much that we used to produce.
How could we equip an army? Would we say what's the use?
I do feel our people still have the right stuff,
But in the modern world is this enough?